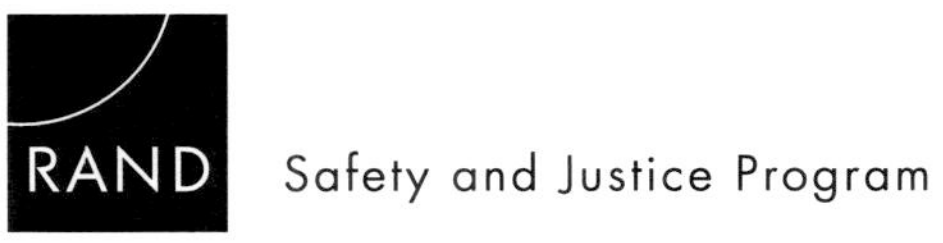
Safety and Justice Program

Effective Policing for 21st-Century Israel

Jessica Saunders, Steven W. Popper, Andrew R. Morral,
Robert C. Davis, Claude Berrebi, Kristin J. Leuschner, Shira Efron,
Boaz Segalovitz, K. Jack Riley

Sponsored by the Israel Ministry of Public Security and
the Younes and Soraya Nazarian Family Foundation,
and donors to the RAND Israel Public Policy Fund

The research described in this report was sponsored by the Israel Ministry of Public Security and the Younes and Soraya Nazarian Family Foundation with additional funding from the Rosalinde and Arthur Gilbert Foundation, the Glazer Family Foundation, and Mr. Stanley Gold as donors to the RAND Israel Public Policy Fund. The research was conducted as part of the RAND Israel Initiative in the Safety and Justice Program within RAND Justice, Infrastructure, and Environment.

Library of Congress Cataloging-in-Publication Data is available for this publication.

ISBN: 978-0-8330-8093-6

The RAND Corporation is a nonprofit institution that helps improve policy and decisionmaking through research and analysis. RAND's publications do not necessarily reflect the opinions of its research clients and sponsors.

Support RAND—make a tax-deductible charitable contribution at www.rand.org/giving/contribute.html

RAND® is a registered trademark

Cover photo: iStockphoto/Thinkstock

RAND OFFICES
SANTA MONICA, CA • WASHINGTON, DC
PITTSBURGH, PA • NEW ORLEANS, LA • JACKSON, MS • BOSTON, MA
DOHA, QA • CAMBRIDGE, UK • BRUSSELS, BE
www.rand.org

Preface

Israel has changed dramatically since its founding, especially in the past two decades. There is a public interest in having the police provide a type and level of service that keeps pace with these changes. Despite relatively low crime rates, the public in Israel perceives an increasing threat to personal security and concern over quality of police service. The Ministry of Public Security, the Ministry of Finance, and the Israel Police asked the RAND Corporation to conduct a study that would help these organizations address several issues of mutual concern. They requested that RAND address issues of public perceptions and public trust in the police, in terms of benchmarking the police against other police organizations, performance measurement, and deterrence and crime prevention. This document reports the outcome of the resulting two-year project.

The project was jointly funded by the government of the State of Israel and with the generous support of donors to RAND's Israel Public Policy Fund, most notably the Younes and Soraya Nazarian Family Foundation, without whose assistance this project would not have been possible. RAND also benefited from generous support by the Rosalinde and Arthur Gilbert Foundation, the Glazer Family Foundation, and Mr. Stanley Gold. This report should be of interest to the public, civil society organizations, and the government of the State of Israel, as well as to those with a general interest in policing policy, police governance, performance measurement, and police-community relations. The study represents one of a series of studies produced by RAND for the benefit of the people and government of Israel as part of RAND's Israel Initiative.

The RAND Israel Initiative and the RAND Safety and Justice Program

The RAND Israel Initiative provides Israeli government clients with analyses of policy options to address major domestic issues in Israel, particularly those related to safety, development, infrastructure, and sustainability.

The research reported here was conducted in the RAND Safety and Justice Program, which addresses all aspects of public safety and the criminal justice system, including violence, policing, corrections, courts and criminal law, substance abuse, occupational safety, and public integrity. Program research is supported by government agencies, foundations, and the private sector.

The RAND Israel Initiative and the RAND Safety and Justice Program are part of RAND Justice, Infrastructure, and Environment, a division of the RAND Corporation dedicated to improving policy and decisionmaking in a wide range of policy domains, including civil and criminal justice, infrastructure protection and homeland security, transportation and energy policy, and environmental and natural resource policy.

Questions or comments about this report should be sent to the project leader, Steven W. Popper (Steven_Popper@rand.org). For more information on the RAND Israel Initiative, see http://www.rand.org/jie/centers/israel.html or contact the director (ii@rand.org). For more information about the Safety and Justice Program, see http://www.rand.org/safety-justice or contact the director (sj@rand.org).

Contents

CHAPTER THREE
**Understanding How Other Police Forces Approach Key
    Policing Issues**

CHAPTER FOUR
Recommendations for Enhancing the Effectiveness of the

Figures

Tables

Summary

Israel has a single, national police force designed to serve all the country's communities. The Israel Police provides the usual services expected of a domestic police force, including patrols and crime prevention, investigation, and prosecution, as well as a host of national services that in other countries, such as the United States, are the province of other agencies.

Israel has changed dramatically over the last several decades, and the police, their governmental partners, and the public desire that policing services keep pace with these changes. To that end, the Ministry of Public Security, the Ministry of Finance, and the Israel Police enlisted the RAND Corporation's Center for Quality Policing to aid in addressing some concerns that have been expressed both by and about the Israel Police. The formal project was overseen by a steering committee of those three bodies, chaired by the Ministry of Public Security. The central question for the effort as a whole was: "What must the police do to provide effective policing to 21st-century Israel?"

The project included assessments of public sentiment about the police, analysis of police deterrence activities, international comparisons for benchmarking and assessment, and recommendations for implementation. Formal analytical activities were balanced with frequent extended visits to Israel, during which RAND staff received briefings on almost all aspects of policing; met with the staff of various specialized police units throughout the country; visited stations and district headquarters; rode patrol in both urban and rural regions; and met with police, Ministry of Public Security, and Ministry of Finance working groups.

Conceptual Model of Effective Policing in 21st-Century Israel

A key concept underlying these analyses is that effective policing depends not solely on the activities or efficiency of the police, but also on the connection between the police and the community being served. As shown in Figure S.1, effective policing requires both *good policing outcomes* and *public support.*

Policing outcomes, as indicated by crime rates, solving crimes, and measures of the level of public order in society, are influenced by many factors other than policing (e.g., socioeconomic status, individual characteristics). The ability to achieve such outcomes will depend in part on how much support the public provides the police. Thus, even if the police judge policing outcomes to be successful according to formal measures of policing, public acceptance and recognition of these outcomes are needed for the police to be deemed *effective* by the citizenry they serve. Without that support, even diligent pursuit of policing tasks may not achieve outcomes deemed satisfactory by all.

Understanding Public Perceptions of the Israel Police

We examined public perceptions of the police, including sources of public dissatisfaction, to establish the foundation for our discussion

Figure S.1
Conceptual Model of Effective Policing in 21st-Century Israel

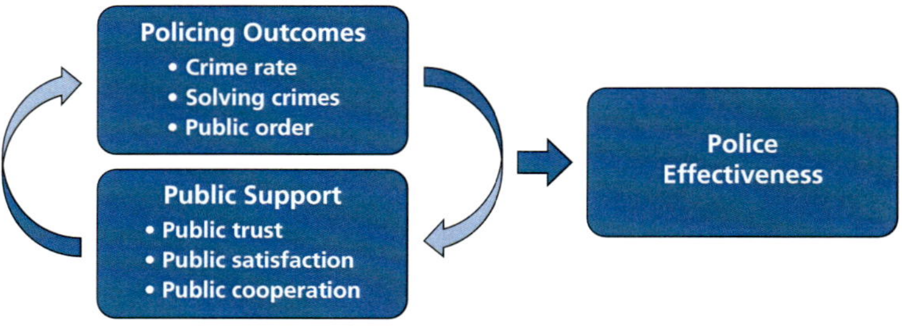

RAND *RR287-S.1*

of policing approaches and recommendations for improving the overall effectiveness of the Israel Police. Relevant tasks included interviews with key informants, a systematic analysis of media content, and focus groups with diverse communities of Israeli citizens. Findings from these analyses reinforced some key messages.

First, the public recognizes many positive elements in police actions and behavior. For example, many sources noted that the Israel Police is effective at fighting many types of crime. The media review found evidence that the police's efforts to improve their image and to increase public satisfaction are finding their way into the press. Sources also expressed the belief that the police need more resources.

At the same time, the public holds many negative views of the police. The perception persists that the police do not always appear to behave in a professional way and do not adequately provide safety and security. Informants noted that the police typically do not have a "customer service" orientation when dealing with the public (e.g., they arrive late, do not write down information). There was also perceived bias in police behavior, and many focus groups described fear of the police. Further, while positive stories about the police found their way into the media, a single negative incident (several of which occurred during the course of this project) could quickly overshadow all improvement efforts. All told, these findings suggest that the Israel Police needs a more effective strategy for developing and maintaining public support.

How Other Police Forces Approach Key Policing Issues

The Israel Police is ususual in many respects, owing to its national organization, the breadth of missions it is responsible for, and the highly heterogeneous composition of the country at the community level. Any solutions adopted for policing tasks in Israel must be tailored to the circumstances in which they will be applied. Nevertheless, it is appropriate for the police to ask, as they have, what options are employed elsewhere to conduct similar missions and carry out comparable activities.

In collaboration with the Israel Police, we identified policing practices from other countries to investigate:

Minority policing. Several countries, including the United States, South Africa, Northern Ireland, Australia, and the United Kingdom, are making concerted efforts to address minority policing issues. Typically, these countries use a combination of approaches, including diversification of the workforce, cultural sensitivity training, and formal antiracism policies.

Implementing responsive and effective policing. Police forces have deployed many new tools in recent decades to improve policing outcomes and their relationship with citizens:

- *Community policing* includes mechanisms for partnership with the community, approaches for problem-solving, and restructuring or realigning the organization to better address the other two components.
- *Problem-oriented policing* emphasizes new and preventive approaches. A problem-solving method widely used by U.S. police agencies is the SARA (scan, analyze, respond, assess) model, which offers a systematic method for focusing police resources on high-priority policing problems and learning from past efforts to address them.
- *Deterrent policing* intersects with community policing in its focus on partnerships with external organizations. General deterrence is aimed at the population level, while focused deterrence is aimed at the segment of population at higher risk of criminal activity (i.e., targeting crime-prone areas and people more closely tied to criminal activity), and specific deterrence is oriented toward the highest-risk segment, people known to be involved in criminal activity. We found that in Israel, as in other countries, the general approach to deterrence of crime is rarely as effective or efficient as a more focused deterrence approach that makes the fullest use of information and analysis to apply policing resources to specific problems and goals.
- *Police volunteers* are used around the world for a variety of purposes, including front office support, traffic control, and search

and rescue. While there are many benefits to using police volunteers, these need to be weighed against the potential costs. There are many common challenges to using volunteers, including police acceptance of volunteers, organizational costs, privacy concerns, and how the conduct of volunteers reflects on the police themselves.

Recommendations

Our overarching recommendation is that the Israel Police adopt a *procedural justice* model of policing to affect public support. This would involve adopting a set of strategies to increase the transparency of police activities and accountability for police performance. We also advocate reducing the use of general deterrence and using more *focused deterrence* to enhance policing outcomes.

A Procedural Justice Model of Policing

Research has shown that when members of the public believe they have been treated fairly, when procedures and decisions are explained to them respectfully, and when they believe their concerns have been heard, they are more likely to assess an interaction with the police positively, *even when the outcome of the interaction is not favorable to them*. More generally, when the public understands police procedures, believes these procedures are fair, and believes the police are being held accountable for their actions and performance, police departments enjoy greater public support. Importantly for Israel, such an approach also makes the role of the police clearer to the public, so expectations can be more closely aligned with policing practices.

While there are many potential paths to implementing procedural justice, we group the actions the Israel Police can take into two broad areas:

- **Demonstrate fair and just procedures:** All citizens are treated according to established procedures, regardless of who they are and regardless of who the responding police officer is.

- **Demonstrate public accountability:** Police are responsible for monitoring their own performance and ensuring that their behaviors are just and fair. Information about police performance is made available to the public so they can judge police fairness themselves.

Increasing procedural justice and transparency means that the Israel Police needs to do a better job at helping people understand what the police do, understand how the police operate, and make informed assessments of the police. The Israel Police has already taken steps to make its procedures and decisions understandable to the public and to establish a system of accountability for the police. We believe that further improvements are possible and will be rewarded with improved public satisfaction, better policing outcomes, and a more efficient policing enterprise in Israel. We provide recommendations in three areas related to procedural justice: (1) performance and accountability, (2) transparency and community engagement, and (3) workforce.

Measuring Police Performance for Accountability

The Israel Police has a new, state-of-the-art performance measurement system, the Mifne, which will be useful for evaluating performance at the station and district levels. We propose some approaches to expanding the Mifne to better focus on outcomes related to public satisfaction with policing performance.

Survey the public's satisfaction with police services to understand the types of interactions that remain a problem for the Israel Police. Involuntary contact surveys gauge the attitudes of people who are stopped by the police for a traffic infraction or for questioning while on foot. For example, in the United States, the Police-Public Contact Survey provides detailed information on the nature and characteristics of face-to-face contacts between police and the public, including the reason for and outcome of the contact.

Survey the culture of integrity at each district station and use the results to target training and other management interventions. Climate and culture surveys assess the environment of integrity within police commands by gauging the level of tolerance for deviating from police codes of ethics. An objective measurement of integrity pioneered by Carl Klockars assumes that police within a force share not only a common set of rules and standards for behavior but also a common culture based on the shared codes of conduct and expectations of agency leadership (Sauerman and Ivkovic, 2008).

Systematically examine field outcomes of interactions between police and the public to flag and investigate episodes of unprofessional or unwanted behavior. Successful transformation of policing cultures requires changes to training and to the assessment of officer performance. For example, a major component of recent reforms at the Los Angeles Police Department was changing the training system to focus more on professionalization. To reinforce this training, the department conducted extensive data collection and monitoring of police performance in the field. Careful monitoring of officer behavior and outcomes can be invaluable for detecting problems and for conveying to officers that they are accountable for their actions.

Develop a performance monitoring system to evaluate individual police on competence, responsiveness, manners, and fairness. It is also important to hold officers accountable for their competence, responsiveness to citizen concerns, manners, and fairness (Mastrofski, 1999). Video recordings of interactions between police and the public offer a particularly rich source of information about individual professionalism (Ridgeway et al., 2009). Moreover, simply knowing that interactions may be subject to later video review and assessment can have a powerful effect.

Improving Israel Police Transparency, Community Engagement, and Responsiveness

Provide the public with detailed crime and police performance data. The media and focus group analyses conducted by RAND demonstrated that the police receive credit from the community when they are successful and when the police take steps to improve their performance. This credit only occurs, however, when the public is made aware of police efforts and achievements. On the other hand, when failures occur or are perceived to occur, the public discourse reverts to themes of police incompetence.

These observations suggest the value not just of increasing transparency about ongoing Israel Police reform efforts but also of providing the public with detailed information about crime and crime trends, as well as about police performance (such as response times, crimes solved, and other performance data). This information would support better-informed and less reactive discussion about community safety and police performance. Social media tools could be used to highlight achievements, point to improving trends, or explain how police are revising their approach to address ongoing or worsening problems or performance. Research evidence suggests that providing accurate information about crime, even when it is high, leads to higher public satisfaction with the police.

Explore options for civilian oversight. A range of independent civilian oversight authorities have been used worldwide to improve the accountability and transparency of departmental management and to conduct evaluations. These arrangements include independent civilian complaint review boards, as in New York City; the establishment of government offices of independent police oversight, as in Los Angeles; hiring a civilian lawyer to serve as the chief of internal investigations, as has been tried by the Seattle Police Department; or use of formal independent monitors charged with investigating and reporting on police activities of greatest concern to the public, such as use of force, bias in stops or arrests, and other police conduct.

If the concept of oversight is considered as a *partnership* with one or more external bodies to enhance police credibility, it becomes a tool that can improve transparency and build the public's confidence that police are accountable for their actions, that unprofessional behavior is not tolerated, and that leaders are taking the steps needed to improve the culture and performance of their departments.

Workforce Modernization

RAND was not asked to assess workforce issues directly as part of its research. Nevertheless, several of the topics RAND was asked to analyze led back to issues related to the quality and professionalism of police personnel. These issues are grouped here under the rubric of "workforce modernization."

Ensure that police and supporting staff are trained in interacting with the public. By instructing officers in *how* to be more open, transparent, and respectful, the Israel Police can increase the level of public satisfaction with the way involuntary interactions are handled. For example, a study in Queensland, Australia, found that drivers had more confidence and trust in police conducting a traffic stop if the police officer provided information on the rationale for the stop and described police procedures (Tyler, 2004; Tyler and Wakslak, 2004; Centre of Excellence in Policing and Security, 2013).

Train and manage police volunteers. Steps should also be taken to make better, more efficient use of volunteers, while ensuring that they are not put in positions where inexperience and lack of formal training will reflect poorly on the Israel Police. This holds special relevance in Israel because police volunteers dress like (and so are indistinguishable from) professional police. It is especially important for the police to develop a clear mission statement and goals for the use of a volunteer police force. Already, Israel Police volunteers are differentiated in terms of those who perform elite functions and those who provide other types of services. For all volunteers, the Israel Police should communicate performance expectations and provide feedback. For those in more-elite positions with time commitments, the police should also hold regular performance evaluations. The effectiveness of both volunteers and *shacham*, or national service recruits serving with the police, should be monitored and evaluated continually.

Apply a strategic perspective to police personnel requirements. Police staffing should be in accordance with the goals that Israel expects its police to achieve, the missions they are asked to carry out, and the activities they engage in to carry out these missions and achieve these goals. Issues of appropriate numbers, categories of personnel, and employment conditions can only be determined on this basis if the Israel Police is to maintain the effectiveness that it expects from itself. In particular, the police should consider a careful analysis of police job functions, to possibly realign personnel resources with departmental strategic objectives.

Improving Policing Deterrence

We also advocate a shift from general deterrence to more *focused deterrence*. This shift would need to be based on specific, structured changes within the organization. These strategies are consistent with initiatives already under way in Israel to implement problem-oriented policing, community policing, and deterrence strategies.

Design focused deterrence interventions. Focused deterrence, when conducted properly, involves forming partnerships with community members and organizations and can necessitate structural realignments to be effective. In short, focused deterrence activities can be supportive of, and an important component of, community policing. For example, the SARA approach has been used against a wide variety of problems, including the operation of open-air drug markets, homeless encampments in urban areas, bicycle theft, neighborhood noise, and gang crime (Center for Problem-Oriented Policing, 2011). Many accessible and helpful training materials for police departments are widely available (Clarke and Eck, 2003).

Create a best practices database. The police in Israel already possess extraordinary potential for deploying existing assets in a way that can take fullest advantage of their abilities to gather and assess data. The efforts the Israel Police has already made to integrate data on activities, performance, and results put it in a good position to go one step further and entertain the possibility of creating its own internal research-based best practices archive.

Next Steps

These recommendations are amenable to phased introduction over time. Table S.1 shows examples of both immediate and longer-term actions for creating a procedural justice model. The steps are derived directly from our recommendations. Table S.2 does the same for focused deterrence.

It is our conclusion that taking such steps will provide both Israel and its police with meaningful assurance that policing effectiveness may be enhanced and maintained in the years to come.

Table S.1
Steps for Adopting a Procedural Justice Model

Outcome	Short-Term Actions	Longer-Term Actions
Ensure that all procedures are fair, unbiased, and transparent	Review and standardize policies and procedures	Release policies and procedures to the public to demonstrate fairness
	Change policies and procedures that are biased	Create system to allow public to monitor police actions; incorporate into Mifne
	Review training and ensure that police standardize their procedures	
Take steps to administer procedures in a fair, unbiased, and transparent way	Train police to administer fair, unbiased, and transparent treatment	Release data on policies and procedures to demonstrate they are being implemented in a fair, unbiased way
	Monitor actions on the street	Release data on individual police accountability; incorporate measures into Mifne
	Create a system of rewards and punishments to incentivize police to use standards	

Table S.2
Steps for Adopting Focused Deterrence

Outcome	Short-Term Actions	Longer-Term Actions
Create new SARA-based deterrence focus at the district, subdistrict, or station level	Form new team to create and oversee project	Conduct research on effectiveness of different deterrence projects
	Train commanders in SARA (or other research-based problem-solving procedure)	Incorporate measures into Mifne
	Submit proposals and hold commanders accountable	
Create a research-based best practices database	Collect data from all projects to identify which projects, and which project components, are successful	Disseminate information on effective programs
		Encourage commanders to use effective practices identified in research
		Incorporate measures into Mifne

Acknowledgments

The authors thank the Younes and Soraya Nazarian Family Foundation, without whose generous gift this project would not have been possible. The Los Angeles–based foundation, with a regional office in Tel Aviv, undertakes charitable giving with the aim of being a catalyst for change. We also thank the Rosalinde and Arthur Gilbert Foundation, the Glazer Family Foundation, and Mr. Stanley Gold—generous donors to the RAND Israel Public Policy Fund—for helping us complete the nongovernmental portion of the project funding. Before he left RAND in May 2012 to join the National Institute of Justice, Greg Ridgeway played a key role as the initiating co–principal investigator and architect of the RAND project.

The following RAND colleagues provided their specific expertise to produce background papers as part of this project: Lila Rabinovich, Emma Disley, Kirsten Keller, Jeremy Miles, Chaitra Hardison, Sarah Greathouse, Dmitry Khodyakov, Luke Gribbon, and Ben Baruch. Janet Garcia and Kashea Pegram of Rutgers University assisted in coding focus group transcripts. Rotem Kadosh and Maor Shay of Hebrew University assisted in coding the body camera video clips. David Kunkel, former chief of the Dallas police, accompanied the RAND project team to Israel to lend his experience in framing this project.

This report benefited considerably from detailed and insightful formal reviews by RAND colleague Ryan A. Brown, Badi Hasisi of Hebrew University, and Ronald Weitzer of George Washington University.

Finally, the authors would like to thank the members of the Ministry of Public Security, the Ministry of Finance, and, of course, the many members of the Israel Police, without whose collegiality, generosity, and effort this project would not have been possible. We offer our special thanks to MG (retired) David Krause, who initiated the project; BG Yaakov Mevorach, without whose help we could not have achieved success; and Mr. Danny Krivaa, who skillfully kept the project on course from the initial discussions, through inception, and on to conclusion.

Abbreviations

DPP   District Policing Partnerships

IDF   Israel Defense Forces

SARA   Scan, Analyze, Respond, Assess

CHAPTER ONE

Introduction

The Israel Police

Since the founding of the State of Israel, the police have been a single, national police force organized to serve all communities. The Israel Police not only provides domestic policing and crime prevention, but also polices the borders; provides traffic, highway, drug, alcohol, and firearms patrols; is the agency for criminal investigation; conducts anti-corruption investigations; operates the national emergency call center; is responsible for domestic counterterror operations and maintaining the national emergency crisis center; administers and manages Civil Guard volunteers; and prosecutes more than 80 percent of all cases in the criminal courts system.[1] Policy oversight of the police comes most directly from the Ministry of Public Security, which also oversees the fire and prison services, as well as several other community-based programs.

The police currently have an authorized strength of 29,300, although the actual force size is below that level.[2] There are no civilian employees of the police.[3] Approximately one-quarter of the total number of police are short-term recruits performing alternative national service. Of the total police force, one-quarter constitute the border police

---

[1] All the figures on police organization and staffing cited in this chapter were provided directly by the Israel Police.

[2] In December 2012, the population of Israel was just under 8 million people.

[3] This share was always small, never more than 5 percent.

force (*Magav*), as distinct from the blue-uniformed police.[4] (Two-thirds of the alternative national service recruits serve in the Magav. Those who serve with the regular police are referred to as *shacham*.) The police also augment their assets by using civilian volunteers who perform both routine and specialized functions under the direction of professional police. Approximately 36,000 volunteers are on the official rolls, although many do no more than the mandatory two half-shifts per month.[5] The police have a system of command that corresponds to that of the Israel Defense Forces (IDF), with the commissioner of police enjoying a rank equivalent to that of the IDF Chief of Staff. Of the commissioned officers (i.e., subinspectors and above, the equivalent of second lieutenants in the IDF), many enter the force as such without having previously served in the lower ranks of the police.

Need for This Study

The police in the past several decades have come under the scrutiny of both the general public and government oversight bodies, particularly the Ministry of Finance and the Ministry of Public Security. As Israel has changed dramatically during this time, there is interest in having the police provide a type and level of service that keeps pace with these changes. The general effectiveness of the police has been questioned, and the apparent high variability in service delivery is a cause for concern, especially in some Israeli communities viewed as underserved by the police. Despite having crime rates in most categories lower than those for similar crimes elsewhere, the Israeli public perceives an increasing threat to personal security. This is matched by concern within the government over the effective use of resources.

---

[4]   Sometimes called the "green" police because of their military-style uniforms, the Magav are also used inside Israel, for example, for patrolling the Old City of Jerusalem.

[5]   A greater level of commitment is required from volunteers performing more-specialized or critical functions. Specialist units, such as underwater recovery and canine or rural horse patrols, are formed entirely from volunteers. During the Second Intifada, after 2001, the number of volunteers was double the current total. Today, about two-thirds of the volunteers wear police uniforms, while the rest perform neighborhood security functions.

Popular approval of the police is lower than that of the IDF and many other public institutions (Hermann et al., 2012); the media's readiness to expose police errors does little to enhance police stature. Within the government, there has long been recurring debate over the adequacy of funding for the police, on the one hand, and the police's ability to use available resources effectively and efficiently, on the other.[6]

RAND's Tasks Supporting the Israel Police

Beginning in 2009, the Division of Strategy and Plans within the Israel Police; the Planning, Budget, and Monitoring Division of the Ministry of Public Security; and the Budget Division of the Ministry of Finance entered into conversations with RAND Corporation staff on how RAND, combining an external perspective and expertise in policing policy, might be able to help address some of the concerns expressed both by and about the Israel Police. It was agreed that bringing analysis to several aspects of the policing problem might provide a means by which the police themselves could move to the next level in taking an active and leading role in addressing public concerns. As shown in Table 1.1, this analysis would include basic research, provide international comparisons for benchmarking and assessment, and yield recommendations for implementation. A formal project began in late 2010 and was overseen by a steering committee chaired by the Ministry of Public Security and including the Ministry of Finance and the Israel Police.

The RAND effort was designed to provide a focused study of distinct aspects of policing in Israel, rather than a comprehensive overview. That said, the topics selected for the study were chosen because it was believed that they would provide entry points for concretely addressing several of the factors that are most troubling to the police themselves and to their public critics. Part of this effort would be to

---

[6] The European Social Survey, 2010, shows that Israelis are the least satisfied with their relationship with the police in comparison to 20 European countries. This was accompanied by a low level of trust in the police. Israel was ranked third from last, with a score of 4.72, better only than Bulgaria and Russia.

Table 1.1
Tasks and Subtasks Included in RAND's Israel Police Research

1	**Public Satisfaction/Public Trust**
1.1	Review of public media sources
1.2	Key informant interviews among academia, media, and nongovernmental organizations
1.3	Analysis of police-public interactions using deployed officer body cameras
1.4	Collection of data on views of the police in community focus groups
2	**Benchmarking**
2.1	Benchmarking with synthetic comparison community
2.2	Review of community policing models
2.3	Review of minority policing experience
2.4	Review of international experience with volunteers
2.5	Review of international experience with emergency phone services
3	**Performance Measurement**
3.1	Review of international practices
3.2	Review of existing and prospective performance measurement systems
3.3	Comparison of proposed performance measures to international practice
3.4	Review of value-for-money: Balancing investments in policing with outcomes
3.5	Review of involuntary contact and culture/climate surveys
3.6	Analysis of Israel Police's Voluntary Contact surveys
4	**Aspects of Deterrence**
4.1	Decomposing deterrence
4.2	Deterrence effects based on time since last police patrol
4.3	Randomized foot patrol experiment design

illuminate how other police forces around the world approach similar policing issues. Thus, the steering committee outlined four broad areas of focus for study:

- public perceptions of and trust in the police
- benchmarking police assets
- performance measurement
- deterrence of violent crime and crime prevention.

Within each of these areas, several specific tasks were selected. The central question for the effort as a whole was: "What must the police do to provide effective policing to 21st-century Israel?"

In conducting its work, RAND needed to be cognizant not only of being external to the police and the other steering committee members but also of coming from outside the country. On the one hand, RAND was asked to provide an objective, external perspective based on its experience with police forces elsewhere. On the other, the project team needed to gain an understanding of the nature of policing in Israel and the unique challenges facing the Israel Police. Therefore, over a period of two years, the formal analytical activities discussed in this report were balanced with frequent extended visits to Israel, during which RAND staff received briefings on almost all aspects of policing; met with the staff of various specialized police units throughout the country; visited stations and district headquarters; rode patrol in both urban and rural regions; and met with police, Ministry of Public Security, and Ministry of Finance working groups selected to represent both headquarters and field, and specialists and line personnel, for each of the main tasks of this project. The discussion that follows is based not only on the formal evidence presented, but also on the experience and understanding we gained from these interactions.

Improving the Effectiveness and Efficiency of the Israel Police

Addressing the overarching question—What must the police do to provide effective policing to 21st-century Israel?—first requires defining what constitutes effectiveness in these terms. Figure 1.1 illustrates the framework that ties together the several tasks of the RAND project

Figure 1.1
Conceptual Model of Effective Policing in 21st-Century Israel

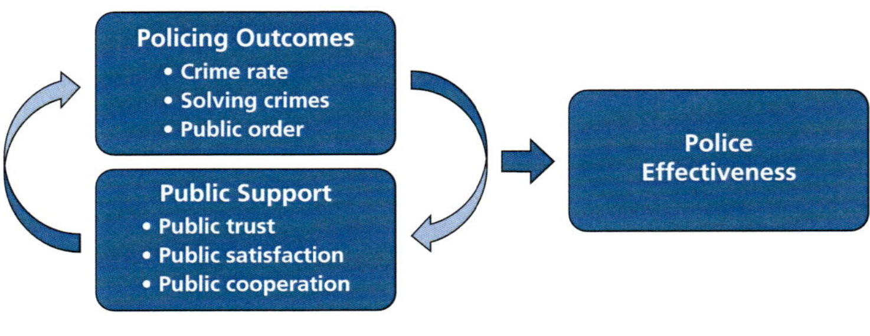

RAND *RR287-1.1*

and also provides a basis for understanding the discussion and findings that are presented in this report.

Effective policing is the result of many factors. It is dependent not solely on the activities or efficiency of the police, but also on the connection between the police and the community they serve. Effective policing requires both good policing outcomes and public support.[7]

Policing outcomes, as indicated by crime rates, solving crimes, and measures of the level of public order in society, are influenced by many factors other than policing (e.g., socioeconomic status, individual characteristics). First, the ability to achieve such outcomes will depend in part on how much support the public provides the police. Second, even if the police judge policing outcomes to be successful according to formal measures of policing, public acceptance and recognition of these outcomes are needed for the police to be deemed *effective* by the citizenry they serve. Thus, even if the crime rate is low overall, a lack of trust or cooperation on the part of the public can mean that the police are perceived as being ineffective.

Thus, if either policing outcomes or levels of support are judged to be insufficient—for any reason—the police will likely be considered ineffective. In this sense, a recurrent claim, such as "the police do nothing about car theft," is important even if the rates of car theft

---

[7]   There are also other forces, such as budgets and crime rates, that we have omitted from the figure for the sake of clarity.

have declined substantially. Such claims provide evidence about the sources of public dissatisfaction, and, in turn, these discoveries can lead to strategies for improvement, perhaps by both improving responses to car thefts and conditioning public perceptions and expectations.

The last point above is important: Effective policing will require a congruence of views on precisely what the role of the police should be in contemporary Israel and how their response to the demands placed on them should be judged. Israel's society is among the most heterogeneous in the world. The police, as a national force, are often the most tangible representation of government that most people see on a daily basis. As the discussion of our findings will show below, perhaps neither party to this intersection has fully understood what the other expects.

Organization of This Report

This document aims to provide an integrated roadmap toward effective policing in Israel. We report in depth on the tasks and aspects of the project that are essential to building public confidence in the police. Ultimately, some of the subtasks were delivered more as technical assistance or were not directly relevant to developing the roadmap. Examples include discussions of emergency call centers, measuring value received from investment in the police, and international comparisons of police performance measurement.[8] We cover these subtasks less thoroughly in this report to keep the focus on how the Israel Police can more effectively carry out its tasks and build confidence with the public.

The remainder of this report is divided into four chapters:

- Chapter Two focuses on public perceptions of the Israel Police.
- Chapter Three considers how other police forces around the world approach key policing issues.

---

[8] The last topic was presented early in the project and led to recommendations that the Israel Police has already implemented in the design of the performance measurement system unveiled in 2012. Therefore, this topic will not be discussed at length in this report.

- Chapter Four provides recommendations for enhancing the effectiveness of the Israel Police.
- Chapter Five provides our conclusions.

Understanding Public Perceptions of the Israel Police

In this chapter, we examine public perceptions of the police, including sources of public dissatisfaction, to establish the foundation for our discussion of policing approaches and recommendations for improving the overall effectiveness of the Israel Police. As discussed in the introduction to this report, public attitudes toward the police are a critical factor in determining policing effectiveness. When the public is supportive and trusting of its police force, people are more willing to cooperate, share information, and assist in ensuring successful policing outcomes. Without that support, even diligent pursuit of policing tasks may not suffice to achieve outcomes deemed satisfactory by all.

Several public opinion surveys support the view that public satisfaction with the police is low in Israel. Vigoda and Mizrachi (2012) shows that the public's satisfaction with the police is the lowest among the 19 public services measured and declined in both 2011 and 2012. This followed three years of modest improvement between 2008 and 2010. The public's trust in the police and the prison service is significantly lower than the public's trust in the IDF and the secret services. Yogev (2010) also documents that public attitudes toward the police are poor compared to other institutions, but also registered some improvement between 2007 and 2010.[1]

The most recent annual index by the Israel Democracy Institute showed that those who replied they had trust in the police to a large

---

[1]   See Vigoda and Mizrachi (2012), pp. 20, 21, and 29; Yogev (2010), pp. 48–59.

extent or to some extent totaled 60.6 percent for Jewish and 62.3 percent for Arab respondents (Hermann et al., 2012).[2] Ben-Porat and Yuval (2009) documents the poor trust levels in the police among Arab Israelis, but also show that the Arab population is interested in improving its relationship with the police and is hoping for improved services better suited to the Arab sector's needs.

In light of these findings, we sought to understand what motivated these expressions of relatively low satisfaction and trust. We examined public attitudes toward the police in four ways:

- We identified and interviewed key stakeholders and opinion leaders across Israel, exploring their attitudes toward the Israel Police.
- We analyzed thousands of stories appearing in the Israeli media that focused on crime and policing.
- We conducted focus groups with diverse communities of Israeli citizens to assess their views of the police.
- We examined videotapes of interactions between police and citizens collected by police officers who agreed to wear cameras for this purpose.

In this chapter, we provide an overview of what we learned about public perceptions from these studies and discuss the implications for the Israel Police.

Key Informant Interviews

Interviews with key informants provide a window into what trained (although not necessarily objective) observers think about the police. Our interviews focused on journalists who cover crime and police-related issues, workers in nongovernmental organizations, and policing scholars. We interviewed 14 people across the three categories. Interviewees were identified through the Israel Police Spokesman's office, as

---

[2]   Interestingly, while only 20 percent of Jews trusted the police to a large extent, the corresponding number for Arab Israelis was 25.1.

well as through independent channels. We asked these informants a set of questions about how the public views the Israel Police and where they think these views originate.[3]

Key Informants Gave Harsh (Though Not Necessarily Objective) Reviews of the Police

Three broad themes emerged concerning the sources of dissatisfaction with the police. First, informants articulated public concern about police professionalism. Some reasons cited for this perception were that police officers are often rude and unconcerned about everyday crimes and that they do not look authoritative. The police typically do not have a "customer service" orientation when dealing with the public (i.e., they arrive late, do not write down information). Second, informants noted that the public sees lack of equal treatment as common among the Israel Police. Interviewees said this stems from a perception that the police often see Arabs only as criminals and ignore them as victims of crime. Most crimes do not get attention unless they are high profile. However, most informants characterized the police leadership as being "fair" in that they desire equal treatment. This is in contrast to the police on the street, whom they perceive as being more likely to conduct themselves inconsistently. Third, while key informants indicated that Israelis generally have a low opinion of the police, they also noted that this is rooted in a general dislike of government institutions. They said that, in general, Israelis are apprehensive about authority, so in this regard, the informants did not distinguish their dislike for the police from that for other government institutions.

Conclusion

The key informant interviews provided initial insights into the public-perception problem facing the Israel Police. We explored these concepts further using the methods described in the next section.

---

[3] Interviews were conducted on a non-attribution basis by several RAND team members but with one member of the team present at all interviews to ensure consistency. The purpose of the interviews was to identify main themes so interview notes were neither formally coded nor subjected to formal analysis.

Media Analysis

Media analysis can shed light on how the discussion of an issue is framed, whether a certain organization is considered a topic worthy of front-page news, and what messages are being sent or ignored by different types of media outlets. This understanding can be used to identify strategies for improving relationships between the police and the local community. Most people have not been victims of crime and may only rarely interact with the police; thus, mass media stories about crime and policing play a key role in forming their impressions of police competence and fairness.

It is common for the media to sensationalize their stories about the police. For example, as Yanich noted in his study of Baltimore and Philadelphia, although murder accounts for a small fraction of all crimes, it dominates in media reporting (Yanich, 1998).[4] Similarly, stories highlighting police abuse of authority can result in negative shifts in public attitudes toward the police (Weitzer, 2002). However, while such biases can significantly influence perceptions of public safety and policing effectiveness, these effects do not necessarily reduce public confidence in the police. Stories can also highlight police successes in ways that reinforce community support for police departments (McCombs, 2004, p. 1).

To assess how Israeli print media portray the police, RAND conducted a systematic media content analysis. The team focused on different types of newspapers—national, local, religious, Haredi,[5] Arab, and Russian—covering a broad spectrum of society. Table 2.1 shows the newspaper classifications and examples for each.

Police-related news items are collected by Ifat, an Israeli press service. Each news article that contains the word *police* is recorded. The police provided RAND with news clips collected between February 23 and May 10, 2012.

---

[4]   Yanich's analysis shows that murder accounts for less than 1 percent of crime in Baltimore and Philadelphia but generated more than 50 percent of the local television reporting. Graber (1980) found similar, albeit less stark, patterns in Chicago.

[5]   The term *Haredi* refers to the ultraorthodox communities in Israel, some of which reject the legitimacy of the state and its authority on religious grounds. The plural form is *Haredim*.

Table 2.1
Newspaper Classifications and Examples

Classification	Examples
National	*Haaretz, Yediot Aharonot, Ma'ariv, Israel Hayom, Israel Post*
Local	*Kol Hasharon, Kochav Nesher, Yediot Modi'in, Lev Hasharon, Ma Nishma Be'eilat, Chadashor Haifa Ve'Hatsafon, Ha'ir Eilat, Sharon Chadash, Shavshevet, Merkaz Ha'Inyanim, Ha'Shavua Be'Ashdod, Chadashot Hakrayot, Zman Krayot, Yediot Ha'Negev, Yediot Hadera, Yediot Ha'Mifratz, Kol Ha'Ir*
Religious	*Makor Rishon, Olam Katan*
Haredi	*Ha'Mevaser, Misphacha—Chadashot Shel Ha'Tsibur Ha'Haredi, Yated Ne'eman, Ha'Modia, Ha'Machane Ha'Haredi, Ba'Kehila, Ha'Eda*
Arab	*Al-Iam, Al-Akhbar, Al-Arabi, Khadith Al Nas, Al Atchiad, Al Quds, Al Usbua Al Arabi*
Russian	*Vesti, Kol Hasharon in Russian, Loch*

Of the initial 6,000 articles provided, 3,492 were directly related to the police, whereas the rest only mentioned the police. We coded the articles directly related to the police by the tone of coverage (positive, negative, or neutral). The breakdown of the items according to their classifications is shown in Table 2.2.

Table 2.2
Breakdown of News Items According to Type and Tone of Coverage

	National	Local	Haredi	Religious	Russian	Arab	Total	Percentages
Positive	12%	26%	13%	20%	7%	7%	622	18%
Negative	18%	12%	14%	18%	15%	31%	553	16%
Neutral	70%	62%	73%	62%	78%	62%	2,317	66%
Total	1,276	1,397	315	202	148	154	3,492	100%
Percentage	37%	40%	9%	6%	4%	4%	100%	

The Local Press Contained the Largest Share of Police-Related News Items

We found that most police-related news articles appear in local press (40 percent), followed by national papers. Exposure was only minor in the sectorial press (Haredi, religious, Arab, and Russian). The frequency with which police-related news appears in local papers may be partly due to the quantity of these papers, which outnumber any other category. Local papers often have pages dedicated solely to police-related news items. Local papers typically cover stories about meetings between police leadership and heads of municipalities, police outreach to the community, police volunteering, and news from local courts.

Most Police-Related News Items Were Neutral, with No Detectable Tone

The majority of police-related news items (66 percent) were neutral in character, with no detectable positive or negative tone. Most articles were succinct, rather dry reports on recent events, usually criminal news. With that said, local media tended to have more positive stories (26 percent), while only 12 percent of stories in national media were positive, and 18 percent were negative. The Haredi and religious media had nearly equal shares of positive and negative items: 13 percent of articles in the Haredi papers were positive and 14 percent negative; 20 percent of articles in religious papers were positive and 18 percent negative. The Russian papers were more polarized, with only 7 percent positive items and more than twice as many (15 percent) negative items. The Arab press is the most polarized, with 7 percent positive stories and 31 percent negative.

Analysis of Themes in Media Stories Echoed Informed Opinions

To identify themes, we then randomly selected articles from each type of publication, in proportion to the share of each type in the full set of articles. The media analysis identified the major themes underlying the reporting on police-related news and examined their recurrence and variance in different types of papers. The themes identified in the papers echoed those described in the key informant interviews.

Positive Themes Focused on Police Strengths

The review identified six broad positive themes.

Renewal and Change

This theme refers to changes in command, appointments, new police stations, new systems, and initiatives. The theme recurred in four of the different types of papers—in all except for the Haredi and Arab papers.

Effectiveness and Preparedness

This theme encompasses successful operations, reduction of crime rates, prevention of terrorist attacks and pro-Palestinian events, and professionalism. This theme appeared in all papers except for the Arab press. In the Haredi press, this theme was manifested mostly in reports about how the police facilitate logistics surrounding Jewish religious events, rather than in relation to fighting crime.

Calls for Increased Forces

This theme was expressed mostly in the national and Arab papers. Despite the vast differences between these types of outlets, both argued that, to restore public order and reduce the crime rate, a stronger police presence is needed, in terms of both resources (e.g., personnel, hours, equipment) and authority. However, while the Arab press emphasized crime in the Arab sector and the need to reduce the number of car accidents in and around Arab towns and villages, the national press gave more attention to combating crime in general and curtailing violence at sporting events.

Nationalistic Priorities

This theme was found mostly in the religious, Haredi, and, to a certain extent, the Russian papers. The theme was expressed in stories about the police vehemently fighting crime in the Arab sector, tackling illegal construction by Bedouins, and preventing pro-Palestinian demonstrations. In these connections the police were commended for their tough stance.

Consciousness (Haredi and Arab)

When police behaved in a way that aligns with the view of the particular sector, it was noted in the press. Thus, for example, when the police prevented a Jewish parade on Temple Mount or when police safeguarded a high-profile visit to the site by an imam from Egypt, it was reported positively in the Arab press. In the Haredi press, on the other hand, police consciousness was noted for sensitive handling of cases within their community.

Awards, Decorations, and Relations with the Community

These stories appeared mostly in the local papers and focus on regional events and awards.

There Were Four Broad Negative Themes

The review also identified four broad negative trends.

Making Mistakes

Negligence is a theme that appeared in all but the religious and Haredi papers. All stories referred to incidents in which police were in error (e.g., not showing up at crime scenes, lying, stealing arms). In the Arab papers, police "failures" typically involved Arab citizens or Palestinians.

Waste or Inefficient Use of Resources

The theme appeared only in national and religious papers. In both, the theme encapsulated criticism, mostly voiced by the State Comptroller, over the police's inefficient use of resources and failure to provide effective service to the public.

Lack of Public Trust

In the national news, this theme broadly captured a general loss of public trust in the police and a deteriorating sense of personal safety, but the religious, Haredi, and Arab papers adopted more of a sectorial outlook. In the Arab press, this theme referred to police failure to address crime in Arab towns. In the religious and Haredi papers, the focus was on the police's evasion of a perceived responsibility to stand by the Jewish side in Arab-Jewish conflicts in Jerusalem.

Excessive or Unjustified Use of Force

Local papers addressed this theme, primarily in relation to police "brutality" in and around soccer stadiums. The Haredi press focused on police violence geared toward Haredi protesters, while the Arab papers blamed the police for scaring Arab civilians and being insensitive.

Comparison of Media Sources Provides Useful Insights into Public Perceptions

There are some limitations to this analysis. First, the printed papers encompass only a fraction of the media to which the Israeli public is exposed. Second, of the Russian papers in Israel, Ifat provides access only to three (*Vesti*, *Kol Hasharon b'Russi*, and *Loch*). Third, although the sectorial papers provide a good indication of overarching trends, it is important to remember that their publics, with the possible exception of the Haredim, also read the daily national Hebrew papers. Despite these limitations, the analysis does yield useful insights for the Israel Police to consider.

Police were both praised and disparaged for the same actions by different groups. The most striking contrast in news coverage shows up between the religious and Haredi papers and the Arab ones. These three demographic groups are most challenged by mainstream Israeli society and are more predisposed to interpret events in terms of this conflict. Interestingly, all three commended the police for their consciousness when their group's narrative was adopted and their needs were addressed in the way they saw fit. However, when the police did not respond as desired, police were vilified as inconsiderate, cowardly, and evading their responsibilities.

A range of themes concerning the police were presented in the sectorial papers. The mix of themes found in each publication type is shown in Table 2.3. The Haredi press was primarily focused on its communities' issues, paying special attention to police handling of sensitive cases and cooperation with the community. The religious papers covered a broad range of topics, including renewal, change, and improvement of police systems and services, waste and inefficient use of resources, and negligence and ineffectiveness. The Russian press shared an "anti-Arab" tone with the religious and Haredi press, though it published little police-related news. The Arab press bore most similarity to the Haredi one in the sense that it was sector-centered. Aside from political issues—namely, Jerusalem, Palestinian prisoners, and

Table 2.3
Most Common Themes, by Type of Publication

	Positive	Negative
National	• Renewal and change • Calls for increased forces • Effectiveness	• Waste or inefficiency • Making mistakes • Lack of public trust
Local	• Renewal and change • Nationalistic priorities • Effectiveness	• Waste or inefficiency • Lack of public use • Excessive or unjustified use of force
Haredi	• Nationalistic priorities • Effectiveness • Consciousness	• Waste or inefficiency • Lack of public trust • Excessive or unjustified use of force
Arab	• Consciousness • Calls for increased forces	• Making mistakes • Lack of public trust • Excessive or unjustified use of force
Russian	• Renewal and change • Effectiveness • Nationalistic priorities	• Making mistakes

the Arab-Israeli conflict—the Arab press seemed mostly concerned with crime in Arab towns, both positively and negatively. The national daily press was interested in broader police-related news. As such, it described efforts to change and improve police systems side by side with the State Comptroller's criticism over waste of public funds. Similarly, it commended the police for successfully executing sophisticated undercover operations with diligence and patience, while at the same time reporting on police failures and mess-ups resulting in a deteriorating sense of personal safety.

Positive stories found their way into the media but could be overshadowed by a single negative incident. Overall, the media review found evidence that the police's efforts to improve their image and to increase public satisfaction are finding their way into the press. Reports on new initiatives, in-depth interviews with police leadership, and sensible responses of police leadership to criticism all gave an impression of genuine endeavors to improve. However, a single negative incident (several of which occurred during the course of this project) could quickly overshadow all improvement efforts.

Interestingly, the Arab press called for more police involvement in Arab towns and villages to help reduce crime. In some instances, it praised police efforts in that regard. At the same time, some commentary in Arab papers acknowledged growing police involvement in combating crime in their sector but criticized the manner of that involvement.

Conclusion

Clearly, the police can have only limited effect on underlying sectarian biases in Israel and, therefore, on how performance of some of their tasks will be reflected in the media that serve Israel's various communities. However, it is possible to stay aware of and be sensitive to these biases and to try to address fairness in public reports about police performance. This understanding can help the Israel Police identify strategies for improving relationships with the various communities and identify stories to promote. The challenges for the police remain twofold: First, negligent behavior should be reduced and gradually eliminated. At the same time, the police need to continue efforts to improve public satisfaction with their performance so that, in the long run, the positive offsets the negative. This can come only from a deeper understanding of the sources of dissatisfaction. To gain this understanding, we turned to focus groups.

Focus Group Analysis

The main messages described in the previous section were reinforced in a series of focus groups with different segments of Israeli society. Focus groups allowed us to explore people's feelings about the police in more depth, in particular addressing the following questions:

- What do different groups of people believe about the police?
- Why do people hold these beliefs?
- How can police improve their relationships with the public?

Importantly, a focus group is not a survey; it provides qualitative, not quantitative, information. While a focus group cannot help judge the *prevalence* of different public attitudes toward the police, it can provide useful insights into *why* some members of the public feel the way they do. The focus group format is designed to elicit emotions, perceptions, and beliefs from a range of individuals. However, it is not designed to achieve balance, even at the individual level. Not all participants will speak at equal length.

We conducted 26 focus groups to delve deeply into police satisfaction and trust within a sample of Israelis to understand where the problem(s) come from and how they may be addressed. In selecting focus group participants, we ensured that a variety of views were represented.

There are documented differences in perceptions of the police and satisfaction with the police by different racial and ethnic groups in Israel (Hasisi and Weitzer, 2007). Therefore, we organized the focus groups to understand differences in perception by ethnicity, gender, and geography. We sampled different racial and ethnic groups across the different regions, including (1) the Tel Aviv metropolitan area; (2) cities outside Israel's center—namely Be'er-Sheva, Jerusalem, and Haifa, which account for 17 percent of the population; (3) villages in both the north and the south. In all, we conducted 28 focus groups, each comprising six to eight interviewees and a trained interviewer who conducted the discussion in the language each group preferred (Hebrew, Arabic, or Russian). Each group met for 90 minutes. Participants received a small stipend for their participation. RAND wrote all questions and procedures.[6] Figure 2.1 depicts the demographic and geographic makeup of each group.[7]

---

[6]   Each focus group was recorded and then fully transcribed into both Hebrew (if not the original language) and English. The English-language transcriptions were coded into NVivo software by two doctoral students in criminal justice from a U.S. university, who independently coded each transcript according to a key provided by the RAND research team. The only portion of the subsequent analysis discussed in this report was conducted by two RAND researchers.

[7]   The Arab and Haredi focus groups were separated by gender, both to respect cultural norms and to reduce the potential of inhibitions caused by group dynamics. The other focus groups were mixed gender.

Figure 2.1
Demographic and Geographic Makeup of Focus Groups

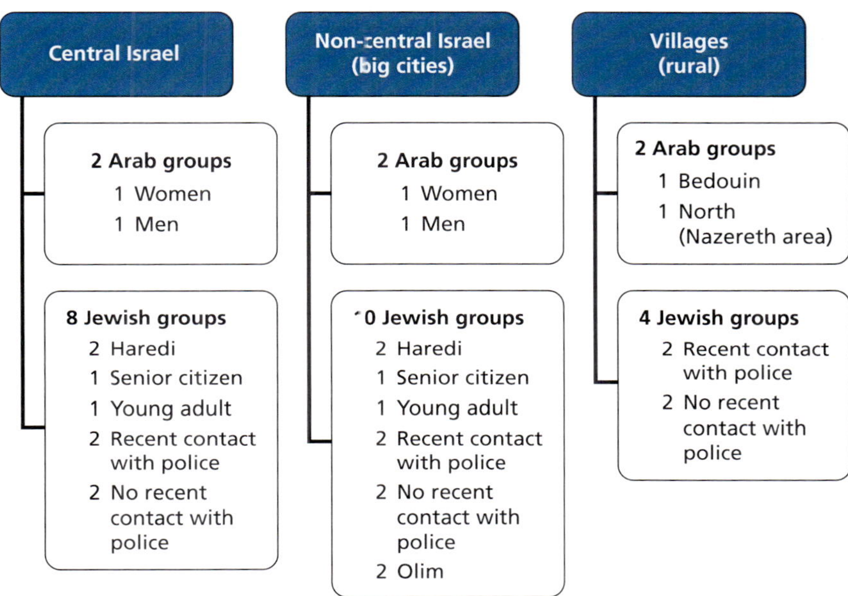

Participants Identified What They Wanted to See in a Police Force

Seven main themes emerged from asking what the police should do (serve the community, demonstrate power and authority, maintain public order, decrease crime, be trustworthy, treat people fairly, respond to calls). Common themes across ethnic and religious groups emphasized preferences for police who are more respectful, empathetic, and sensitive to cultural factors. In addition, there was a desire for more-effective policing services, including faster responses to calls for service and greater attention to (or perhaps impact on) security. Even the views that narrower segments of the sampled communities expressed—i.e., that the police need to appear more serious or that they should treat everyone equally—appear broadly consistent with the emphasis on improved policing professionalism expressed by all groups.

Focus group participants said that officers varied greatly in their level of professionalism. Indeed, a consistent theme across all but the

Olim main groups was that the treatment people receive from the police is largely determined by the specific officer with whom they interact. Similarly, *olim*[8] and Arab respondents suggested that police behave differently with citizens depending on the citizen's ethnicity or such factors as the type of car the citizen drives.

There Were Areas of Disagreement Among Different Groups, Including Fear of Discrimination and Fear of the Police

Members of the Jewish community emphasized that they want the police to serve the community and demonstrate power, while the olim emphasized that the police should demonstrate power and also keep order and treat all equally. Arab focus groups emphasized beliefs that the police assert the power of the state and that their actions promote inequality. Haredim said that the police should be more involved with the community. Arabs said that they often feel targeted by the police because of their ethnicity. Haredim and even secular Jews also said that they feel targeted, not because of their ethnicity but for other reasons, such as so the police officer can fill his or her quota of tickets or because the citizen talked back.

Many focus groups described fear of the police. Arabs said that they fear police because of racism, while Jews said they were afraid of potential consequences, such as receiving a costly ticket. Many Haredim said they fear police officers even if they have not had a bad experience with the police—e.g., "You see a cop, you see a threat."

Participants Held Diverse Views on the Factors That Determine How a Person Is Treated by the Police

Focus group participants also had varying ideas about what determines the way a person is treated by the police, as shown in Table 2.4. For Arabs, ethnicity is viewed as the one determining factor. As one focus group participant said, "We are a second-class people, and we are aware of the fact that we do not receive first-class services." Most

---

[8]   The term *olim* refers to new Jewish immigrants to Israel. A significant share of the current population of Israel is represented by the nearly 1 million arrivals from the former Soviet Union after its dissolution.

Table 2.4
Focus Group Responses to: "Which Factors Determine How a Person Is Treated by the Police?"

	Other Jewish	Haredim	Olim	Arab
Depends on the citizen's ethnicity				X
Depends on the individual police officer	X	X		X
Depends on the citizen's vehicle			X	X
Depends on the citizen's behavior	X			X
Depends on the situation	X	X		
Depends on other demographics	X			

NOTE: An "X" indicates items mentioned at least once in the focus groups for this ethnic group.

groups emphasized, however, that treatment depends on the individual police officer's personality and disposition. Citizens' behavior and the specifics of the situation were also frequently cited.

Focus Groups Identified Desired Changes

Focus groups also identified the types of improvements they would like to see, as shown in Table 2.5. Among the most desired improvements were to see the police be more respectful and more empathetic, to make citizens feel safer, and to increase awareness of cultural issues.

Conclusion

Overall, the focus groups emphasized that perceptions of the police differ by ethnicity, consistent with the findings of the sectorial media analysis. Some differences reflect different interaction patterns between police and demographic groups. Some differences reflect differences in opinions of Israel and the Israeli government. But it is striking that there is a concern about respect and treatment across all groups, even those in the majority. Dissatisfaction stems from a dissonance between the roles people believe the police should play but do not or cannot.

Table 2.5
Focus Group Responses to: "How Should the Police Change?"

	Other Jewish	Haredim	Olim	Arab
More respectful/better treatment of citizens	X	X	X	X
More attentive/empathetic	X	X	X	
Faster response times	X	X		
Appear more serious	X			
Make citizens feel safer; attention to security	X	X		X
Treat everyone equally				X
Awareness of cultural issues		X	X	X

NOTE: An "X" indicates items mentioned at least once in the focus groups for this ethnic group.

Analysis of Police Interactions with the Public Using Data from Compact Video Cameras

Interactions between the police and public, especially negative ones, have been linked to attitudes about the police. Compact video cameras have made it possible to document public interactions. While cameras have not yet been widely adopted for routine police department use, several instances point to their diagnostic value in addressing issues of police doctrine and policy. For example, U.S. police departments, including Austin, Texas, and Oakland, California, have begun pilot programs that place small body cameras (e.g., attached to a lapel or hung on a lanyard) on police personnel. The intention is that the cameras will help build evidence in cases, prevent witnesses from retracting statements, and document the actions of the police.

As an experiment, the Israel Police agreed to equip six officers from each of the Petach Tikva and Ayalon stations with body cameras for a period of two weeks. As a condition for undertaking this pilot, police were allowed to turn the cameras on and off at their discretion. As a result, a complete record of interactions with citizens may not have been collected. There were 112 clips totaling 10 hours of video that were judged to be usable, although only 20 percent contained a complete interaction from start to finish.[9] Further limiting the generalizability of the sample, the police prescreened every clip before sharing them with the research team to filter out clips judged to pose possible legal questions either for the police or for privacy protection. This creates an unknown bias in the final sample of clips. One-half of the resulting sample of clips were from traffic stops, and another one-quarter resulted from citizen complaints or calls for service.

Clips were coded by native Hebrew speakers following written guidance from RAND on how to code their content. The coding focused on seven main factors:

- characteristics of the officer and other individuals involved in the interaction
- description of the interaction
- how the police presented themselves
- how the police communicated with the others
- how others communicated with the police
- how the police explained procedures
- perceived public satisfaction with the interaction.

Cameras Recorded Many Positive Interactions Involving the Police

The sample of clips represented in this data set revealed reasonably successful interactions. In 75 percent of all recorded interactions, police officers were rated as being in control of the situation. In 68 percent of clips, the officer was judged to have listened to the citizen's complaint or explanation; in 53 percent of the clips, the officer explained to the

---

[9]   To be deemed usable, a clip needed to be over 30 seconds long and allow us to both hear and see the interaction sufficiently to code it. Native Hebrew-speaking trained coders, who were also graduate students in criminal justice in an Israeli university, performed the actual coding using a manual provided by RAND. Owing to the limitations under which this experiment was conducted, and that its principal purpose was not analytical but rather to acquaint the Israel Police with this approach so as to evaluate its potential usefulness within Israel based on direct experience, we did not require independent coding by the two coders and relied upon their analyses.

citizen what was happening. Perhaps not surprisingly, these recorded interactions appeared relatively satisfactory for citizens. In 65 percent of the cases, the citizen was judged to be respectful to the officer, and in only about 33 percent of the clips did the citizen express dissatisfaction with the interaction. As we discuss below, research shows that this is one of the most important aspects of an interaction that leads to satisfaction.

The findings in Israel are not inconsistent with other places. For example, Ridgeway et al. (2009) examined videotapes of motor vehicle stops in Cincinnati and found that police ended the interaction on a positive word in 65 to 75 percent of the cases, depending on the race of the motorist.

There Were Also Several Negative Interactions

In 25 percent of all interactions, police were judged to have engaged in an argument with some member of the public. Citizens appeared to view the police officer as working to resolve the problem in fewer than half of all clips (43 percent), and coders judged that the police were trying to resolve the problem in only 60 percent of the clips. Citizens were judged to be satisfied in just one-third of the interactions with another third showing no clear positive or negative indications.

Summary

Because of the way in which the camera experiment was conducted, it was neither intended nor expected to provide strong conclusions. Nonetheless, cameras provide anecdotal evidence to suggest that, even when police are respectful, interactions frequently become argumentative and disrespectful. Although it has been widely demonstrated that explaining police procedure is a key factor affecting satisfactory outcomes, police failed to do so in about one-half of all interactions. Finally, citizens often leave interactions without believing that the officer tried to resolve the problem.

Chapter Conclusion

Public perceptions might differ from the results of an objective assessment of data. Yet an understanding of such perceptions not only provides a key to engaging the public more effectively on the themes that concern them, it enables the police to craft strategies that can increase the public support component of effective policing.

Combined, the findings discussed in this chapter reinforce the same messages. The public recognizes many positive elements in police actions and behavior. For example, the Israel Police is effective at fighting many types of crime. There is also a belief that the police need more resources. At the same time, the public holds many negative views of the police. The perception persists that the police do not always appear to behave in a professional way and do not adequately provide safety and security. There was also perceived bias in police behavior. All told, these findings suggest that the Israel Police needs a more effective strategy for developing and maintaining public support.

Understanding How Other Police Forces Approach Key Policing Issues

The project steering committee requested that RAND perform several tasks to provide benchmarks on how other police forces around the world approach selected policing issues. Short reports were provided on each requested topic. In this chapter, we highlight some key findings from these efforts, focusing on topics that will provide a foundation for our findings and recommendations. First, we report on an effort to compare Israel Police operations to those of police peers in U.S. communities with similar demographics and policing needs. Second, we discuss other countries' approaches to policing minority communities and implementing more responsive and effective policing, including community policing. Finally, we describe models and practices for using police volunteers as well as trends in handling emergency calls.[1]

Benchmarking the Israel Police Against U.S. Police Practices

The Ministry of Public Security, the Ministry of Finance, and the Israel Police have sought to identify international benchmarks that allow comparisons with other countries in terms of crime rates, police

---

[1]   In addition to these topics, RAND also prepared reports for this part of the project on ongoing reforms in the operations and management of emergency call centers, international practices in performance measurement, examples of conducting value-for-money assessments, and review of public satisfaction survey instruments.

force size and structure, costs, and other measures. Such comparisons are challenging, however, given the unique features of each country and its police force. To address this issue, RAND crafted a benchmark that describes what American policing *would look like if applied in Israel*. Because the United States has thousands of law enforcement agencies, we created the benchmark by assembling data from several agencies that collectively have the same population and crime profile as localities in Israel. The Israeli locales, in turn, were selected to make close matches between police station jurisdictions and city boundaries. To make this comparison, we used an approach known as *synthetic control group* statistical techniques (Abadie, Diamond, and Hainmueller, 2010). Using this approach, we were able to identify some differences between the characteristics of the Israel Police force and those of the U.S. synthetic comparison groups.

Of course, Israel faces ethnic and religious strife, bombings, and other challenges distinct from those that U.S. police must confront. In contrast, the United States has one of the highest rates of private gun ownership in the world (estimated at about 89 guns per hundred people, whereas Israel may have just around seven per hundred[2]) (Graduate Institute of International Studies, 2007). These differences, and many others, limit the utility of direct comparisons between U.S. and Israel Police approaches to staffing.[3] Nevertheless, these results provide a different and new point of view for comparison.

We Matched U.S. and Israeli Forces on Predictors of Police Force Size and Composition

The following are the predictors of police force size and composition that we used to match U.S. and Israeli police forces:

- demographics
  - population size

---

[2]   The figure refers to private gun ownership only. Because of reserve duty and civil guard activity, guns are more widely accessible than this figure would suggest.

[3]   Some of these differences include different labor practices between U.S. police forces and the Israel Police and different crime categories and definitions.

    – population size squared[4]
    – percentage of population under age 18
    – percentage of male population under age 18
    – percentage of population over age 65
- crime rates
    – homicide
    – robbery
    – assault
    – burglary
    – auto theft
    – theft.

We identified the weighted combinations of U.S. policing districts that most closely matched the selected Israel Police stations on the items shown in the list.

Using these synthetic comparison groups, we illustrated how U.S. communities might staff and train police departments serving communities with demographics like those matched to individual urban Israel Police stations.

For example, the Be'er Sheva station in Israel has the matched population characteristics described in Table 3.1. Searching across all U.S. policing districts, we were able to identify a weighted combination of U.S. districts that closely matches Be'er Sheva on each of these variables. Table 3.2 identifies the districts contributing to this synthetic comparison sample and their weights or influence on the synthetic comparison.

We validated that all the variables we described above do predict the size of the police force. There are other variables that theoretically could also drive police force size (particularly other sociodemographic characteristics of the population, such as race, ethnicity, or economic indicators), but we were unable to match these across the two countries because they have different meanings. If we could assume that

---

[4] The size and cost of police forces are correlated to the size of the population served or to the size squared. Small towns need smaller forces than big cities, and as force size grows, costs escalate disproportionately (Reaves, 2010).

Table 3.1
Match Between Be'er Sheva and U.S. Synthetic Comparison

Statistic	Be'er Sheva	U.S. Synthetic Comparison
Population (000)	193.4	185.45
percent < 18	0.26	0.26
percent males < 18	0.27	0.27
percent > 65	0.12	0.12
Homicide/1,000 population	0.01	0.01
Robbery/1,000 population	0.73	0.80
Assault/1,000 population	1.51	1.51
Burglary/1,000 population	6.03	5.66
Auto Theft/1,000 population	5.23	4.64
Theft/1,000 population	17.62	18.43

the demographic variables selected for creating these synthetic groups are the key factors determining the size and composition of the force a U.S. community would create to address the policing challenges in Be'er Sheva, we could make a direct comparison of the observed force characteristics for the synthetic comparison group and those actually used in the Be'er Sheva station (Table 3.3).[5]

Comparisons Identified Differences in Policing Approaches

The comparison between the Israel Police and the U.S. synthetic comparison group reveals some structural differences.

Number of Police Inspectors

In Be'er Sheva the authorized and actual numbers of police classed as either intelligence or investigation (105 and 100, respectively) are

---

[5]   Data on U.S. force characteristics were drawn from the Law Enforcement Management and Administrative Statistics dataset collected by the U.S. Department of Justice (2007). Note that this data set does not provide a breakdown according to the same categories used by the Israel Police.

Table 3.2
Weights for the Cities That Make Up the
Synthetic Comparison Group

City	Weight	Population
Chula Vista, California	0.18	215,447
Gilbert, Arizona	0.17	204,904
Vancouver, Washington	0.14	160,826
Henderson, Nevada	0.13	246,369
Scottsdale, Arizona	0.09	233,105
Port St. Lucie, Florida	0.07	145,740
Boise City, Idaho	0.06	202,703
Warren, Michigan	0.05	133,941
Pueblo, Colorado	0.05	103,626
Overland Park, Kansas	0.03	170,216
Casa Grande, Arizona	0.03	38,667

almost twice the expected number classed as investigation officers in the U.S. comparison. This suggests possible differences in the workload and assignments of inspectors in the two countries that may reflect real differences in crime or differences in policing philosophy.

Total Authorized Force

In contrast, the total authorized force of 259 full-time–equivalent officers in Be'er Sheva is only about two-thirds of the total staffing size expected in the comparison U.S. district (including both sworn and civilian full-time employees in the United States). A crucial difference lies in the fact that, while a little more than two-thirds of the U.S. workforce would be sworn officers, with paid civilian staff making up the remainder, in Be'er Sheva and other Israel Police stations, nearly all paid positions are filled with sworn officers. These differences raise questions about, for instance, whether the demand for policing is substantially lower in Israel than in the United States, whether policing is much more efficient in Israel, whether volunteers (not shown in

Table 3.3
Comparing U.S. Synthetic Control to Authorized and Actual Staffing Levels in Be'er Sheva

Category	U.S. Synthetic Control Equivalent Number	Be'er Sheva Authorized Number	Be'er Sheva Actual Number
Sworn full-time employees[a]	267	259	235
Civilian full-time employees	113	0	0
Patrolmen	144	115	96
Investigators	54	65	62
Intelligence		40	38
Traffic		14	14
Community police		13	13
Logistics		6	6
Command		6	6
Operating budget ($ millions)	234		
Academy training hours	749		
Field training hours	728		
Annual in-service training hours	51		
Number of marked cars	108		
Number of unmarked cars	68		

[a] Note that perhaps 10–15 percent of sworn officers in a typical Israel Police station will be shacham.

Table 3.3, but likely numbering 400 or more individuals for Be'er Sheva alone) adequately compensate for the comparatively lower force levels, and whether some staff and support functions currently performed by sworn officers could instead be performed by less-expensive civilian staff.[6]

---

[6]   Some of the number who would be considered sworn officers in the United States would be shacham in Israel. These would cost considerably less than either civilian employees or professional sworn officers. They may well fill the jobs that might otherwise go to civilian

Comparisons for Other Israel Police Stations

We conducted analyses similar to those for Be'er Sheva with data for the Hadera, Petah-Tikva, Mesubim, Zevuloon, Ashdod, Haifa, Ashkelon, Rehovot, Rishon-Lezion, and Glilot police stations. Table 3.4 shows the ratio of authorized staffing for each of these stations to its corresponding U.S. synthetic counterpart. The comparison should be interpreted carefully since, in each instance, actual sworn full-time staffing of the stations in Israel was below the authorized levels used in this comparison, while the numbers used to create the U.S. synthetic comparison group relied on actual staffing. This was reflected most heavily in the difference between authorized and actual levels of officers assigned to patrol. In many stations, the actual level of staffing for investigation and intelligence was equal to the authorized level.

Table 3.4
Ratio of Authorized Staffing of Israel Police Stations to U.S. Synthetic Comparison Group

Station	Total Authorized Sworn Full-Time Employees	Patrolmen	Investigators and Intelligence
Ashdod	0.61	0.52	0.71
Ashkelon	0.88	0.70	2.00
Be'er Sheva	0.97	0.80	1.95
Glilot	0.71	0.69	1.38
Hadera	1.02	1.17	1.79
Haifa	0.85	0.78	0.34
Mesubim	0.64	0.53	1.00
Petah-Tivka	0.75	0.56	1.22
Rehovot	0.78	0.67	1.19
Rishon-Lezion	0.71	0.64	1.08
Zevuloon	0.96	0.79	1.17

employees, with the downside being that their limited term of service would not allow them to become either fully skilled or experienced in some of the office or policing functions they may be asked to fulfill and that the department would lose the knowledge and skills they develop during their tenure upon their departure.

Operating Budgets, Training, and Motor Fleets

Although we did not collect data on the operating budgets, training, or motor vehicle fleets of the 11 Israel Police stations we compared with the U.S. synthetic comparison group, we provided this information for the composite U.S. forces so that Israel Police, Ministry of Public Security, and Ministry of Finance staff could make these comparisons on their own.

Conclusion

Despite the important caveats noted above, differences revealed between the Israel Police force characteristics and those of the U.S. synthetic comparison group may be useful starting points for discussions about whether the real differences in context between the two countries explain differences in the approach each has taken to workforce organization and training and whether there are aspects of the U.S. approach that might be appropriately adopted for the Israeli context.

Approaches to Policing in Minority Communities

The research on policing in general, and on the policing of minority communities in particular, has not received as much attention in Israel as it has in other countries, such as the United States, South Africa, Northern Ireland, Australia, and the United Kingdom. In all these countries, as well as Israel, relations between minority communities and the police have often been strained, and some countries are making concerted efforts to heal these tense relationships. RAND conducted a review of strategies that are being used in other countries to improve relationships in minority communities. We highlight some key findings from this review here.

Minority Policing Needs to Address the Problems of Both Overpolicing and Underpolicing

Existing research indicates that policing of certain minorities is characterized by two simultaneous phenomena, each of which leads to public mistrust and dissatisfaction: (1) the use of aggressive tactics targeting minorities, often referred to as *overpolicing*, and (2) the neglect of minority communities, especially those who are being victimized, which is referred to as *underpolicing*. Minorities who experience one or both of these phenomena are less likely to cooperate with or trust the police, which then feeds back into police misconduct and neglect in these communities.

One of the expressions of police racial or ethnic bias that has received the greatest research attention is the perception that the police actively target minorities and view them as suspects rather than citizens (overpolicing). In many countries, police are accused of using race or ethnicity as a basis for increased suspicion and scrutiny of minority individuals. This is most evident when police stop and search individuals of minority ethnic or racial origin on the basis of their background or appearance rather than suspicious or criminal behavior. Research suggests that members of minority groups are targeted more than majority group members and also shows that, regardless of whether this targeting is actually occurring, it is perceived to be occurring. Research has found that people are more likely to want to cooperate with police when they feel they will be treated in a fair, respectful, and impartial manner and that these perceptions vary significantly between different ethnic and racial groups (Murphy and Cherney, 2012). In the United States and the United Kingdom, ethnic minorities have been found to evaluate law enforcement in much less favorable ways than the majority does (e.g., Cochran and Warren, 2012).

A Variety of Measures Are Used to Address Minority Policing

There are seven main types of action to address policing minorities or policing in diverse societies (Stenning, 2003; Ben-Porat and Yuval, 2011):

- diversification of the police force (which involves changing patterns of recruitment)
- cultural sensitivity training for police officers
- formal antiracism policies within the police
- review and revision of practices that may lead to systematic discrimination against certain groups

- liaison between the police and minority communities (which can be achieved, for instance, through a community policing approach)
- inclusion of minority group representatives within the membership of the police's governing authorities
- retraining on well-vetted police policies.

Although these policies are being implemented in many departments, there is little evidence on the effectiveness of most of these policies.

Evidence is most extensive in relation to diversification of the police force. Stepping up efforts to recruit ethnic minority officers has been one of the strategies used in the United Kingdom, Israel, and elsewhere to redress racism within the police force, improve police treatment of the minority population, and thus improve the public's perception of the police and relations between the police and minority communities (Bowling and Phillips, 2003; Weitzer and Hasisi, 2008). Some evidence suggests that minority police officers may better understand and communicate with minority citizens. For example, one U.S. study found that black drivers are more likely to evaluate police behavior negatively when they are stopped by a white officer, even after controlling for the reported reason for the stop (Cochran and Warren, 2012). However, much evidence also "shows little difference between officers of different racial and ethnic backgrounds in their routine treatment of citizens and suspects" (Weitzer and Hasisi, 2008, p. 363). Evidence from New Orleans and Detroit suggests that diversification of the force (each now has a majority black police force) did little to improve blacks' views of the police, but did reduce whites' confidence (Weitzer and Hasisi, 2008, p. 363).

Systematic Research Is Lacking Regarding Other Practices

There is little systematic evidence on the other practices. For example, the evidence on the effectiveness of diversity training for police officers is not well developed. A small but growing body of research examines the impact of diversity training on workplace inequity, although not specifically on the police. One study from the United States, for instance, examined officers' perceptions of the need for diversity training (Gould, 1997), finding that new recruits tend to be more accepting of this kind of training than experienced officers, who more often saw it as a waste of time. Other studies have examined either the content or the teaching style in police diversity training (Birzer, 2003; Blakemore et al., 1995).

Much of the support for reforms to address minority policing is anecdotal. There is no research on policies that lead to racial discrimination, although it is assumed that ridding organizations of discriminatory policies reduces minority alienation. There is also no evidence concerning the effect of formal antiracism policies, although there is anecdotal evidence of the effect when black officers were introduced into the forces. It is assumed that introducing minority group members to a governing authority helps realign priorities, although studies are needed to support this view.

Conclusion

The collective evidence seems to indicate that no single approach to policing minority communities is a panacea. It is likely that a suite of changes is necessary to improve the relationship between the police and the minority communities they serve. As will be discussed in the next chapter, a procedural justice model of policing, one based on the notion of fair and transparent application of police procedures, shows promise as a means of helping improve relationships between the minority community and police. Such a model incorporates citizen participation during the police encounter, strives for perceived police neutrality in decisionmaking, and emphasizes the need for maintaining dignity and respect.

Methods for Implementing Responsive and Effective Policing

Police have deployed many new tools in recent decades to improve policing outcomes and their standing with the citizenry. Figure 3.1 illustrates the relationships among the concepts we use to discuss these changes, since there is overlap and synergy among them.

Figure 3.1
Relationship Among Policing and Deterrence Concepts

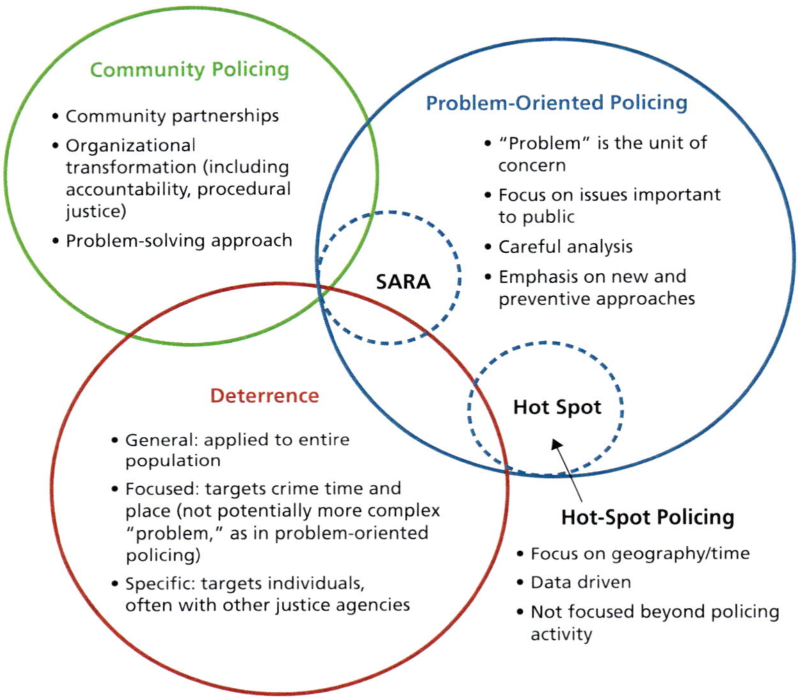

NOTE: Areas of overlap are not scaled to convey the degree of congruence or divergence between concepts.

Community Policing

The concept of community policing comprises three main components: implementing mechanisms for partnering with the community, developing approaches for problem-solving or meeting community needs, and restructuring or realigning the organization so that it can better carry out the first two components. Community partnerships can range from collaboration with other government agencies, the media, and service providers to more-effective inclusion of the business community.

Israel has been implementing some community policing elements, including biannual meetings between local police and city agencies to discuss problems and solutions, the use of *Mashak* (community police officers) in local substations, increased priority given to reducing quality-of-life offenses, and regular meetings between police station commanders and at-risk juveniles. A relatively new program of "municipal patrol" (*shitur yroni*) does hold a prospect for potentially becoming a platform for community policing. In each city where this expanding program has been instituted, a dedicated cadre of police officers is specifically assigned to patrols along with municipal inspectors. Currently, the focus is primarily on quality-of-life crimes and issues such as building-code violations. The specific focus in each case is determined at the local level and targeted to the circumstances of the particular community. As this program expands and its results are assessed, it may become a vehicle for closer police-community cooperation. But at present, the police do not appear to have realigned their organization in support of a community-oriented mission nor developed the deep and extensive community partnerships that are the hallmark of community policing organizations.

The evidence on the effectiveness of community policing in improving relationships between the police and minority communities is still sparse. Some results in community policing are promising. For instance, research has suggested that collaborative police-citizen relationships can improve residents' perceptions of safety and reduce the incidence of quality-of-life offences (Reisig, 2007). Early studies on community policing have also shown that it can reduce fear of crime and improve relationships between the police and the public (Sozer and Merlo, 2012).

Community policing is done either by using specialized community policing officers, such as the Mashak in Israel, or by training all officers in community policing issues and procedures (the so-called generalist approach). Although there are clear theoretical advantages to changing police cultures to adopt a community policing approach to all activities, departments have had difficulty making such a change in practice. In fact, Pelfrey (2004) argues that police departments have typically not achieved a generalist force—even when they have tried to implement one—but instead tend to have officers who assume a community policing (proactive) role and others who perform traditional policing (reactive) duties. This, in effect, produces a specialist community police. Maguire and Wells (2009) indicates that, while generalized community policing has been widely advocated by policing reformers, U.S. police departments appear to have become more, not less, specialized since the 1990s.

Police departments internationally have adopted a range of approaches to implementing specialized community policing services. For example, the Oakland Police Department implemented a community policing program similar to the Mashak that involved deploying one police officer (or problem-solving officer) in every one of the city's 57 beats (Wilson and Cox, 2008). These officers' most common duties are talking with the neighborhood service coordinator, receiving citizen complaints, and making security checks. In 2008, the United Kingdom created a new position in policing—a police community support officer—as part of a neighborhood policing strategy (also called local policing.) The objective is to rebuild trust and confidence between the police and local communities (Raine and Dunstan, 2007; Wakefield, 2007). Dedicated teams of police and police community support officers work together with special constables, local authorities, volunteers, and community partners. Neighborhood police officers provide a visible and familiar presence, working with community members to identify and prioritize local problems and then taking "an intelligence-led, proactive, problem-solving approach to . . . specific local issues" (Home Office, 2004).

A different model is found in Northern Ireland, in which a long history of sectarian conflict has only begun to "normalize" in recent years. In Northern Ireland, District Policing Partnerships (DPPs) were established as part of a move toward community policing in the years following the end of the conflict (Topping, 2008).[7] DPPs had responsibility for consulting, identifying, monitoring, engaging, and acting within the community according to the objectives of the policing plan

---

[7] DPPs were replaced in April 2012 with Policing and Community Safety Partnerships. These are statutory bodies that bring together the functions and responsibilities of DPPs and Community Safety Partnerships (Northern Ireland Policing Board, 2012).

and were thus a tool for the police to reach out and engage with communities. However, observers have noted that DPPs have been challenged by low attendance, political manipulation, biased membership, and a negligible effect on the daily routine of the rank-and-file community police officers (Topping, 2008). Topping (2008) argues that the lessons from the failure of DPPs to engage the community effectively are that "mechanisms for engagement must be conceived as deliberative, 'bottom-up' processes based upon engagement with pre-existing community infrastructures" (p. 789).

Problem-Oriented Policing

In problem-oriented policing, the unit of concern is the defined "problem" that has been identified as being important to the public or in achieving policing missions. Problem-oriented policing is an inherently analytical approach that emphasizes new and preventive approaches. While any specific problem may not require transformation of the policing organization, making this an ongoing, consistent basis for policing activities probably will require changes.

A problem-solving method that is widely used by police agencies in the United States is the SARA (scan, analyze, respond, assess) model, which is used to identify and prioritize problems, understand the root causes of the problems and candidate interventions, implement the best potential interventions, and evaluate the results of the effort (U.S. Department of Justice, undated).

The SARA approach offers a systematic method for focusing police resources on high-priority policing problems and learning from past efforts to address them. When the City of Los Angeles was facing gang-related gun violence that was among the worst in the United States, RAND assisted in supporting a SARA process that resulted in significant, measurable reductions in violence (Tita et al., 2003). After selecting the Boyle Heights neighborhood as the top priority for intervention (through a scanning process), RAND researchers conducted a detailed analysis of available homicide data designed to understand the key features associated with recent crime. Contrary to conventional wisdom, this analysis found that homicides were not generally associated with control over illicit drug markets, but instead resulted from inter-gang tensions related to personal honor or prestige.

Working with police, prosecutors, and community service providers, RAND facilitated a planning effort that designed a dynamic intervention combining both "carrots and sticks" (i.e., incentives and disincentives) to first suppress violence in the neighborhood, then maintain lower violence rates through deterrence measures. Throughout the implementation of the effort, RAND assessed its effectiveness in reducing violence and the fidelity of the implementation to refine the intervention in real time to optimize its results.

Similar SARA model approaches to policing problems have been implemented by police departments without the assistance of research organizations like RAND, and many accessible and helpful training materials for police departments are widely available (e.g., Clarke and Eck, 2003).

Hot-spot policing is a problem-oriented policing method that relies on spatial analysis—mapping—to understand the patterns associated with crime and assist in deciding where and when to deploy police resources. Hot-spot policing may displace crime to other locations or times where it is less damaging, or it may deter the crime, leading to less of it overall.

Deterrence

There are three main forms of deterrence: general, focused, and specific. Deterrent policing intersects community policing in its focus on partnerships with organizations outside the police. It places less emphasis on building community partnerships or reorganizing the police to support the approach. General deterrence is an effort aimed, largely indiscriminately, at the population level. It does not target individuals who may be crime-prone. Focused and specific deterrence are two closely related concepts. *Focused deterrence* is data and geography driven. It typically targets crime-prone areas where significant shares of the population are exposed to crime risk or potentially engaged in criminal activity. *Specific deterrence* is oriented toward people known to have been involved in criminal behavior. The crucial distinction is between general deterrence, which is aimed very broadly, and focused or specific deterrence, which is aimed at areas and people more closely tied to criminal activity.

We performed one analysis of whether general deterrence measures would show a deterrent effect in Israel. The Israel Police collects automated vehicle location records that allowed us to analyze general deterrence resulting from patrol cars passing a location. We used a sample from these records to conduct a series of multivariate logistic regressions to test whether the presence of a patrol vehicle deterred crime. The regressions controlled for such variables as time of day, seriousness of crime, and station location.

We were unable to demonstrate that crime reports were significantly less likely in the time immediately after a car had passed than in the same area either a day or two weeks later. In fact, we found a small but statistically significant increase in reported crime. This may result from police patrolling areas where they correctly anticipate crimes may occur, may reflect some queuing effect (that is, after seeing a patrol car pass citizens might then decide to report crimes that might otherwise have gone unreported), or be due to some other phenomenon.

It is possible that analyses of other data could change this result; failing to detect a general deterrence effect is not the same as demonstrating that one does not exist. But consistent with current views of general deterrence, we found in our tests no evidence of such an effect on reducing crime. In later sections of this report, we discuss more focused approaches to deterrence that might help the Israel Police more effectively achieve deterrence of major crime.[8]

Use of Volunteers

No Organization for Economic Cooperation and Development or European Union country relies as heavily upon police volunteers as

---

[8] Specific deterrence efforts often involve collaboration with other parts of the criminal justice system, such as probation and parole. In contrast, police can typically implement focused deterrence by themselves. Since we did not examine probation, parole, and other criminal justice functions, we cannot comment on the role of specific deterrence, and instead confine our discussion to focused deterrence.

does Israel. RAND was asked to review the use of volunteers in other countries with the objective of drawing lessons that could benefit Israel. The inclusion of citizen volunteers in law enforcement supplements the police workforce and provides an opportunity to strengthen community-police relations. However, there are challenges in effectively using volunteers and ensuring a positive effect on policing outcomes.

RAND examined volunteer practices in eight countries: Australia, Canada, Denmark, the United Kingdom (England and Wales), Germany, South Africa, Switzerland, and the Netherlands. We conducted a systematic search of the volunteer practices described in the academic literature and searched websites of national police forces to extract relevant comparative data to develop an overview of where and how volunteers are used. However, because little detailed information on volunteers was available and because data were difficult to verify, we did not attempt to make precise comparisons between forces.

Here we summarize key observations from our study.[9] In the next chapter, we make specific recommendations for improving the Israel Police's management of volunteers.

Using Volunteers Has Many Potential Benefits

Volunteers can provide important additional manpower and support to law enforcement in a variety of efforts, from providing administrative and front-office functions to participating in community engagement activities and, in some countries, performing traditional law enforcement duties. In Israel, the Civil Guard has been involved in patrolling key public areas, providing traffic control, and carrying out rescue operations, among other functions (Yanay, 1993). For example, all canine units are staffed by volunteers in Israel. Volunteers are used to reduce costs and to free trained police so that they can focus on more serious crime prevention and investigation. Volunteers can also bring important language and technical skills that police agencies need, such as computer expertise, knowledge of complex industries (like banking), or even deep expertise in policing, as when police retirees volunteer.

---

[9]   Many of the points we raise about the potential benefits and risks of law enforcement volunteers are also discussed in other sources. For an example, see Ayling (2007).

Finally, volunteers can be especially valuable in assisting with community engagement and community policing interventions.

Countries Use Volunteers in a Variety of Ways

The review found that models for how to use volunteers are quite diverse across the eight countries. Some key areas of difference are described below.

Authorities

Many countries and jurisdictions give volunteers little authority, while others grant police volunteers power equal to that of police personnel (e.g., Royal Canadian Mounted Police Auxiliary Program, England and Wales, Germany [Baden], the Netherlands, South Africa). In some countries, such as Canada and South Africa, volunteers are even allowed to carry a gun once they have been properly trained. In countries where volunteers do not have full police power, volunteers focus on administrative, investigative, and preventative activities.

Responsibilities

In some cases, volunteers serve more of support function, such as providing front-office and administrative support and assisting with community events (e.g., England and Wales, Australia Federal Police). In other cases, volunteers take a more active role in certain aspects of policing, such as conducting ground patrols, traffic control, and helping in search and rescue operations (e.g., Canada [Royal Canadian Mounted Police], Denmark, Germany).

Minimum and Maximum Time Commitments

Some police forces we profiled, such as those in Canada, England, and Wales, require volunteers to serve a minimum number of hours per month or per year. The Canadian Auxiliary Constable Program requires a minimum of 160 hours per year, and the England and Wales Special Constables are required to volunteer for a minimum of 16 hours per month (192 hours per year). In contrast, other police organizations enforce a maximum number of hours that volunteers can serve. For example, in Hesse, Germany, the members of the *Freiwilliger Polizeidienst* can serve a maximum of only 25 hours a month (300 hours a year).

Pay

Three police forces we profiled offer some level of hourly pay to volunteers. In the Netherlands, the *Vrijwillige Politie* are paid an hourly rate, which was around €6 in 2006. Additionally, they are entitled to one bonus payment per year. In Germany, participants in the Hesse Freiwilliger Polizeidienst can be paid €7 per hour, while in Saxony, volunteers are permitted an allowance of €5.11 per hour. Since 2002, Special Constables in England and Wales can also be paid, but this decision is left to each police force. Some forces pay between £500 and £1,000 a year, while others give Specials Constables a discount on local taxes.

Size of the Volunteer Force

We did not find data on the exact numbers of sworn officers, civilian employees, and volunteers for every surveyed department in the same period. However, public source information we collected suggests that some departments, such as in Denmark, England, Wales, Canada, Brandenburg (Germany), and Australia, have relatively high ratios of volunteers in relation to regular police (ranging from 1:1.78 in Denmark's Police Home Guard to 1:18.40 in the Netherland's Vrijwillige Politie). In other countries, ratios were more in the range of 1:20 to 1:35. Only in Israel are there more volunteers than police, with a current ratio of about 1.3:1, down from a previous level of ten years ago of closer to 3:1.

Uniforms

Apart from Brandenburg (Germany), all volunteers wear a uniform. However, apart from South Africa, the uniform worn by volunteers distinguishes them from regular officers.

Effectiveness of Volunteers Is Unclear

There is little research concerning the use of police volunteers. Most research on volunteers focuses on community engagement and police attitudes, not on the use and effectiveness of volunteers in policing. Although many of the potential benefits of using volunteers are clear (e.g., providing additional manpower and skills, enhancing community relations), there are very few guides as to how effective volunteers are in performing their tasks and how great the benefit is, on balance, from using them.

Police Forces Face Common Challenges in Using Volunteers

There are many common challenges in managing volunteers. These include police acceptance of volunteers, organizational costs, the potential for misconduct, and privacy concerns surrounding volunteer access to information. For example, police may feel their jobs are threatened if they perceive that their primary duties and responsibilities are being taken over by unpaid or lesser paid citizens (e.g., Gaston and Alexander, 2001). Regular police may resent the additional responsibilities involved in training volunteers, worrying about the safety of volunteers, or monitoring the appropriateness of their behavior, meaning that volunteers could become more of a distraction than a benefit. These observations are consistent with historical accounts suggesting that the regular police initially did not accept the Israeli Civil Guard (e.g., Yanay, 1993).

Potential to Undermine Police Credibility

Perhaps the biggest challenge in using volunteers is the potential for them to behave in ways that undermine police credibility and effectiveness. Personal interactions with police and interactions reported in the media are important in shaping public attitudes and satisfaction with a police force (e.g., Brown and Benedict, 2002; Hinds, 2009; Rosenbaum et al., 2005). Because police volunteers can play a significant role in policing efforts, depending on the powers they are granted, they may be viewed by the public as representatives of the police force or be portrayed as such by the media, especially when they are indistinguishable from the uniformed police. As a result, volunteers' actions may be just as important as those of regular police in shaping public attitudes. In this way, ineffective engagement and response or misconduct, such as excessive force or antagonistic interactions with citizens, can jeopardize police-community relations and lower public satisfaction. More-severe abuses of power (such as extortion or sexual assault) may be especially threatening if volunteers appear to have the authority to seize property, issue legal citations, or detain or arrest citizens.

Privacy Concerns

Law enforcement agencies have access to private and confidential information that has the potential to be compromised or misused—not only in their databases, but also in the information collected as part of investigations (Davids, 2008). Depending on how volunteers are incorporated into police activities, they may have direct or indirect access to this private information. Like other instances of misconduct, abuse or leaks of private information have the potential to severely damage public trust and confidence in the police force. Therefore, identifying appropriate activities for volunteers that will not risk the breach of private information is critical.

Conclusion

While there are many potential benefits to using police volunteers, these benefits need to be weighed against the potential costs. Gaining police and unit acceptance is also critical to the success of a volunteer program. In the next chapter, we describe some recommendations for using volunteers effectively.

Chapter Conclusion

The Israel Police is distinctive in many respects, owing to its national organization, the breadth of missions for which it is responsible, and the composition of the country at the community level. Any solutions adopted for policing tasks in Israel must be tailored to the circumstances in which they will be applied. Nevertheless, it is appropriate for the police to ask, as they have, what range of options is employed elsewhere to conduct similar missions and carry out comparable activities. While none of these examples can be blindly accepted without further study on how they may be implemented in Israel, they do provide illumination and the basis for making recommendations for Israel's own police to consider.

CHAPTER FOUR

Recommendations for Enhancing the Effectiveness of the Israel Police

In this chapter, we present the conclusions from our research and from discussions with and observations of the Israel Police in the form of recommendations for enhancing the effectiveness of the Israel Police.

We have two overarching recommendations. The Israel Police should adopt a *procedural justice* model of policing. This would involve adopting a set of strategies to increase the transparency of police activities and accountability for police performance. We also advocate reducing the use of general deterrence and using more *focused deterrence*. This shift in deterrence posture would need to be based on specific, structured changes within the organization. These strategies are consistent with initiatives already begun in Israel to implement problem-oriented policing, community policing, and deterrence strategies.

We detail these strategies by providing recommendations designed to address four issues:

- measuring police performance for accountability
- improving police transparency, community engagement, and responsiveness
- modernizing the police workforce
- improving police deterrence.

A Procedural Justice Model of Policing: Increasing Fairness, Accountability, and Effectiveness

As detailed in this report, public perceptions of the Israel Police are mixed. Although a common motif in public discourse is that the Israel Police is improving and seeking change, it is nevertheless clear that dissatisfaction with police performance is widespread, extending to all segments of Israeli society. Police are frequently characterized as insufficiently competent and unfair, and the quality of police officers is viewed as uneven.

Even though most Israeli citizens may never have reason to interact with the police, when there is a widespread perception that the police suffer from systematic shortcomings and that there are weak individual officers, such sentiments can undermine the cooperation and coordination with communities that are essential to successful policing outcomes. When the public has confidence in a police department, a virtuous cycle results: Good policing and results help build public support, and public support contributes to better policing outcomes.

A key emphasis in these analyses is that effective policing is the result of many factors. It is not solely dependent on the effectiveness or efficiency of the police but also depends on the connection between the police and the community being served.

Figure 4.1 reproduces the framework shown earlier (in Figure 1.1), but now indicates the two categories of recommendations. As previously discussed, effective policing depends on both policing outcomes and public support. A central focus of our work was to understand the public-support component of this framework. The discussion of public perceptions in Chapter Two indicated that the Israel Police needs a more effective strategy for developing and maintaining public support. This is true not only in minority communities but also among the general public.

A procedural justice model is key to building public support for the police in Israel. Procedural justice is not a program or an intervention; it is a model for policing based on the transparency of the criminal justice system and on fairness. Indeed, there are many different variants of procedural justice in policing and the broader criminal

Figure 4.1
Conceptual Model of Effective Policing in 21st-Century Israel, with Recommendations

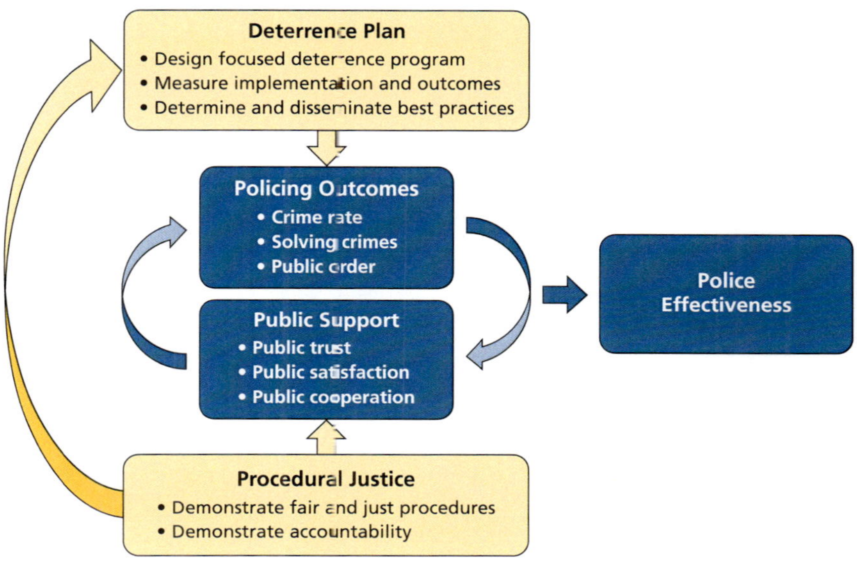

justice system, but three elements are generally common: police require public support and cooperation; support and cooperation are derived from the perceived legitimacy of the police; and perceived legitimacy stems in part from the actions of police (Tyler, 2004). Research has shown that, when members of the public believe they have been treated fairly, when procedures and decisions are explained to them respectfully and when they believe their concerns have been heard, they are more likely to assess an interaction with the police positively, *even when the outcome of the interaction is not favorable to them.* More generally, when the public understands police procedures, believes these procedures are fair, and believes the police are being held accountable for their actions and performance, police departments enjoy greater public support. Importantly for Israel, such an approach also makes clearer to the public what the police role is, so that expectations can be more closely aligned with policing practices.

While there are many potential paths to implementing procedural justice, we group the actions Israel Police can take to increase public support and improve perceived legitimacy into two broad areas:

- **Demonstrate fair and just procedures:** All citizens are treated according to established procedures, regardless of who they are and regardless of who the responding police officer is. Citizens are accorded dignity and respect and allowed to participate in police encounters (i.e., the police actively listen to citizens).
- **Demonstrate public accountability:** Police are responsible for monitoring their own performance and ensuring that their behaviors are just and fair. Information about police performance is made available to the public so that they can judge police fairness. Making such information available—i.e., providing "transparency" into police procedures and behavior—is critical for allowing citizens to draw informed conclusions about the police.

The analysis in Chapter Two suggests that, no matter the actual conditions, the police have not effectively *demonstrated* to the public that both conditions are true.

Different police departments have approached the issue of procedural justice in different ways. Some have provided structured training and established procedures to maintain standards for police behavior in interacting with citizens. Some have conducted reviews of policies and procedures to determine whether they are biased. Departments have also taken steps to ensure that everyone in the organization understands the procedures.

Increasing procedural justice and transparency means that the Israel Police needs to do a better job at helping people understand what the police do, understand how the police operate, and make informed assessments of the police. The Israel Police has already taken steps to make its procedures and decisions understandable to the public and to establish a system of accountability for the police. We believe that further improvements are possible and will be rewarded with improved public satisfaction, better policing outcomes, and a more efficient policing enterprise in Israel.

Measuring Police Performance for Accountability

We recommend that the Israel Police develops and uses performance measures to measure public satisfaction, police integrity, and the performance of individual police. These recommendations are summarized in Table 4.1 and described in more detail below.

Expand Mifne to Include Public Satisfaction and Police Integrity Measures

The Israel Police has a new, state-of-the-art performance measurement system, the Mifne, which will be useful for evaluating performance at the station and district levels. We propose some approaches to expanding the Mifne to better focus on outcomes related to public satisfaction with policing performance.

Surveys are increasingly used to assess policing performance. Many traditional measures of police activity, such as the volume of crime complaints or the number of arrests, are ambiguous and difficult to interpret. For example, if arrests go up, it suggests that police are productive, but are they actually deterring crime? Surveys of commu-

Table 4.1
Recommendations: Policing Performance Measurement and Accountability

Area	Recommendation
Public satisfaction	• Survey the public's satisfaction with police services, using the results to understand the types of interactions that remain a problem for the Israel Police and for which additional training or other management interventions may be required
Police integrity	• Survey the culture of integrity at each district station and use the results to target training and other management interventions to correct cultural norms in any districts found to be out of step with Israel Police objectives for acceptable police behavior
Performance of individual police	• Systematically examine field outcomes of interactions between police and the public to flag and investigate any police officer whose outcome patterns reveal unprofessional or unwanted behavior • Develop a performance monitoring system to evaluate individual police on competence, responsiveness, manners, and fairness

nity residents can produce a more accurate picture of the true rate of crime and can be used to assess the sense of security in the community. In particular, two types of surveys may be especially valuable for the Israel Police to consider: *involuntary contact surveys* to measure public satisfaction with police performance and *climate and culture surveys* to measure police integrity. Ridgeway et al. (2009, pp. 43–48) provides discussion of an internal benchmarking process that can be used to assess the performance of individual officers. Walker et al. (2001) discusses early warning systems that have helped identify potential problem officers.

Involuntary Contact Surveys to Measure Public Satisfaction

Involuntary contact surveys are conducted to gauge the attitudes of people who are stopped by the police for a traffic infraction or for questioning while on foot. Police stops have been blamed in the United Kingdom's Macpherson report (Macpherson, 1999) and elsewhere for creating feelings of ill will, especially in minority communities. This has been used to explain the usual finding of lower satisfaction with police among members of ethnic minority communities (Weitzer and Tuch, 2002). Moreover, new research suggests that the level of satisfaction with involuntary police contact can be improved by greater transparency and by police officers showing respect while making the stop. In a Seattle study, significant differences were detected between white and black respondents who had involuntary police contact (Davis and Hendricks, 2007). Black respondents were less likely to state that police officers treated them professionally, explained the reasons for the stop, had a valid reason for the stop, detained them for a reasonable amount of time, explained any subsequent obligations resulting from the stop, or handled the situation satisfactorily overall. Consistent with other research studies, the Seattle survey found that opinions about the police were shaped less by the fact of an involuntary encounter itself than by the way the police handled the encounter.

The U.S. Department of Justice regularly assesses citizen perceptions of both involuntary and voluntary encounters with the police. The Police-Public Contact Survey is a supplement to the National Crime Victimization Survey, which collects data on crime against persons aged 12 years or older from a nationally representative sample of U.S. households. Respondents are asked about their police contact for the 12 months prior to conducting the survey. The Police-Public Contact Survey provides detailed information on the nature and characteristics of face-to-face contacts between police and the public, including the reason for and outcome of the contact.

Recommendation: The Israel Police or an independent research entity should conduct regular surveys of the public's satisfaction with police services and use the results to understand the types of interactions with the public that remain a problem for the Israel Police and for which additional training or other management interventions may be required.

Climate and Culture Surveys to Measure Police Integrity

Climate and culture surveys are designed to assess the environment of integrity within police commands. These surveys are administered to officers within a police unit to gauge the level of tolerance for deviating from police codes of ethics.

Police integrity has been defined as "the normative inclination among police officers to resist temptations to abuse rights and privileges of their occupation" (Ivkovic and Shelley, 2008). When police violate norms of integrity defined by law or departmental policy, they risk loss of public confidence and respect for the rule of law (Bayley, 2002). Given these high stakes, most police agencies strive to maintain high levels of integrity through selection and training of personnel and the "climate and culture" of the department (Klockars et al., 2000).

While police integrity has been a concern of policing experts over the years, an objective measure of integrity is quite recent. Historically, the most common measure of integrity has been the volume of citizen complaints; however, this measure has been shown to be affected by many factors, especially the ease of filing a complaint (see, for example, Walker, 2005). In the 1990s, an objective measurement of integrity was pioneered in a method that assumes that police within a force share not only a common set of rules and standards for behavior but also a common culture based on the shared codes of conduct and expectations of agency leadership. It is the culture that influences what officers see as acceptable and what they see as deviant (Sauerman and Ivkovic, 2008).

Developed by Carl Klockars, the survey is simple and easy to administer. A set of 11 hypothetical violations of police norms are presented to individual police in a confidential setting. Police rate the case scenarios based on their perceptions of the seriousness of the infraction, expected disciplinary action, and willingness to report the incident. After the survey was given to more than 3,000 officers in 30 police agencies, researchers found "substantial differences in the environments of integrity among the agencies studied" (Klockars et al., 2000, p. 1). Klockars concluded that "adopting the view that integrity is an organizational or occupational responsibility is more effective than emphasizing personal ethics or morality" (Klockars et al., 2005, p. 1). This survey has been used extensively by U.S. and non-U.S. police departments widely viewed as in need of reform (Davis et al., 2010).

Recommendation: The Israel Police should use the Klockars survey, or one adapted for use by the Israel Police, to evaluate the culture of integrity at each district station and use the results of the survey to target training and other management interventions to correct cultural norms in any station found to be out of step with Israel Police objectives for the acceptable behavior of its officers.

Measure the Performance of Individual Officers

Successful transformation of policing cultures requires changes to training and changes to the assessment of officer performance. For example, a major component of reforms at the Los Angeles Police Department in the last decade was changing the training system to focus more on professionalization. To reinforce this training, the department conducted extensive data collection and monitoring of police performance in the field. Such incidents as use of force, police shootings, and complaints were documented more seriously and transparently.

Similarly, in response to complaints of bias among some police, the Cincinnati Police Department and the New York Police Department have evaluated individual performance on a range of outcomes that could reflect unprofessional or unwanted behavior. Comparisons were made among police with similar beats, shifts, and responsibilities. Officers stopping unusually high proportions of persons from a particular minority group, ethnic group, gender, or other characteristics more often than their peers in similar settings were highlighted through this benchmarking system (Ridgeway, 2007).

Members of the police with discrepant outcome patterns are not always engaged in unprofessional behavior. Nevertheless, careful monitoring of officer behavior and outcomes can be invaluable for detecting real problems when they emerge and for conveying the message to all officers that they are accountable for their actions.

Monitoring is essential for performance assessment, but many important features of performance are not likely to be detected in field outcomes alone. It is also important to hold officers accountable for their competence, responsiveness to citizen concerns, manners, and fairness through more comprehensive documentation of police activities and police-citizen interactions (Mastrofski, 1999). Video recordings of interactions between police and the public offer a particularly rich source of information about individual professionalism (Ridgeway et al., 2009). As we discussed earlier, cameras worn by Israel Police officers recorded interactions with the public that could be used to rate the competence and professionalism routinely exhibited by individual officers. Moreover, simply knowing that interactions may be subject to later video review and assessment can have a powerful effect on officer behavior.

Recommendation: The Israel Police should systematically examine field outcomes of interactions with the public to flag and investigate those police whose outcome patterns may reveal unprofessional or unwanted behavior. In addition, the Israel Police should develop a performance monitoring system, such as that suggested by Mastrofski (1999), or the routine use of video recordings of interactions to evaluate officers on their competence, responsiveness, manners, and fairness.

This set of recommendations carries implicit within it the suggestion that Mifne should begin a transition from evaluating *police stations* alone to also evaluating *individual police officers* in areas where it would be relevant to do so. This would also involve tracking field outcomes of interactions and other police activities at the individual level. For the latter purpose, the police should now consider a larger-scale experiment with body video cameras to explore the possibility of using them as part of routine evaluation.

Improving Israel Police Transparency, Community Engagement, and Responsiveness

Recommendations for improving police transparency, community engagement, and police responsiveness are shown in Table 4.2.

Provide the Public with Detailed Crime and Police Performance Data

The media and focus group analyses RAND conducted demonstrated that the police receive credit from the community when they are successful and when the police take steps to improve their performance. This credit only occurs, however, when the public is made aware of police efforts and achievements. On the other hand, when failures occur or are perceived to occur, the public discourse reverts to themes of police incompetence.

These observations suggest the value not just of increasing transparency of ongoing Israel Police reform efforts, but also of providing the public with detailed information about crime and crime trends, as well as about police performance (such as response times, crimes solved, and other performance data). This information would support better-informed, less reactive discussion about community safety and police performance. Social media tools could be used to highlight

Table 4.2
Recommendations: Transparency, Community Engagement, and Responsiveness

Area	Recommendation
Public reporting of police performance	• Provide the public with detailed crime and police performance data, making use of social media or other communication tools to enhance the public's recognition of the efforts Israel Police is making to improve performance
Civilian oversight boards	• Explore options for improving transparency through use of civilian partners to provide credible oversight of police statements and actions

achievements, point to improving trends, or explain how police are revising their approach to address ongoing or worsening problems or performance.

Police forces are increasingly placing more information on crime and police actions in the public domain. In Los Angeles, it is possible to enter an address into an online site maintained by the police and find a mapping of different types of crime within a set radius of that address over a specified period. Some have argued that making such information available may alarm the public, make them feel less secure, or provide useful information to potential lawbreakers. Others have suggested that making information available creates a risk of alienating groups at the ends of the political spectrum. However, in practice, none of these things has occurred as a result of making information available on crime and police actions. Research evidence suggests that providing accurate information about crime, even when it is high, leads to higher public satisfaction with the police. With better information about crime and police performance and with an improved understanding of the Israel Police's commitment to transparency and performance improvement, the public may gain confidence in police leadership and may become more supportive of police efforts.

Recommendation: Provide the public with detailed crime and police performance data, making use of social media or other communication tools to enhance the public's recognition of the efforts Israel Police is making to improve performance.

Explore Options for Civilian Oversight

Implementing the previous recommendation assumes an element of police performance that may be lacking in Israel: the presumption that the police are providing accurate information about their actions. Other Israeli public institutions face similar problems with credibility. However, the RAND study illustrates that the Israel Police's credibility problem extends across all of Israel's communities, not just those outside the majority culture. If public support is to increase, the police need to demonstrate a break with the past that will be perceived as extraordinary.

Like other police departments, the Israel Police performs a public service, paid for by the public, and thus is ultimately accountable to the public. Meeting public expectations requires the department not only to have leadership and management controls that ensure that this public service is performed efficiently and fairly, but also to provide assurance that this is the case. Many large departments in the United States, such as those in New York City, Los Angeles, San Diego, Cincinnati, and Seattle, have found themselves in situations that led the public to become suspicious that the management of police behavior and performance was not sufficiently rigorous or candid to ensure the expected level of service. There is good reason to find similarity with the situation in Israel.

In these cases, a range of independent civilian oversight authorities have been used to improve the accountability and transparency of departmental management and to conduct evaluations. These arrangements include independent civilian complaint review boards, such as exist in New York City; the establishment of government offices of independent police oversight, such as occurs in Los Angeles; hiring a civilian lawyer to serve as the chief of internal investigations, as has been tried by the Seattle Police Department; or use of formal independent monitors charged with investigating and reporting to the public on police activities of greatest concern to the public, such as use of force, bias in stops or arrests, and other police conduct.

If the concept of oversight is considered to be a *partnership* with one or more external bodies to enhance police credibility, it becomes a tool that can improve transparency and build the public's confidence that police are accountable for their actions, that unprofessional behavior is not tolerated, and that leaders are taking the steps needed to improve the culture and performance of the department.

Recommendation: The Israel Police should begin to institutionalize mechanisms for improving transparency through independent, credible oversight of police statements and actions.

Workforce Modernization

RAND was not asked to assess workforce issues directly as part of its research. Nevertheless, several of the topics RAND was asked to analyze led back to issues related to the quality and professionalism of police personnel. In this section, we provide findings and recommendations on workforce training and management that arose during our work. These are shown in Table 4.3.

Ensure That Police and Supporting Staff Are Trained in Interacting with the Public

Ensuring that police officers and supporting personnel interact with the public in a way that supports procedural justice requires setting and maintaining high standards of professionalism and providing appropriate training.

By instructing officers in how to be more open, transparent, and respectful, the Israel Police can increase the level of public satisfaction with the way involuntary interactions are handled. As simplistic as it sounds, an illuminating study in Queensland, Australia, tested whether police could increase the involuntary contact satisfaction level by changing interactions during a traffic stop. Police were assigned

Table 4.3
Recommendations: Workforce Modernization

Area	Recommendation
Training for police and support staff	• Ensure that all sworn police, shacham, and volunteers are trained to interact with citizens in ways that enhance procedural justice
Training and management of volunteers	• Develop a clear mission statement and goals for the use of a volunteer police force • Provide supervision, performance feedback, and accountability • Monitor volunteer and shacham program effectiveness
Strategic assessment of staffing and training polices	• Conduct an explicit strategic study of police goals, missions, and activities and the personnel base that could best achieve them in an ongoing basis • Based on the above, conduct an assessment of the appropriate balance between sworn police, shacham, civilians, and volunteers

either to conduct a stop to administer a breathalyzer test with no further explanation or to explicitly describe to the person detained the procedures the police were following and the rationale for doing so (the "procedural justice" condition) (Tyler, 2004; Tyler and Wakslak, 2004). Resulting surveys showed that drivers assigned to the procedural justice condition thought that police were fairer, had more confidence and trust in the police, and reported higher levels of satisfaction with police than drivers assigned to the control condition (Centre of Excellence in Policing and Security, 2013).

Efforts to enhance public perceptions of the police might grow over time. Research has found that stories heard from friends and family members about police encounters are significant factors shaping people's opinions of the police (Miller et al., 2005). Thus, as people recount their positive experiences to friends and family, these efforts may enhance community opinions of the police even among citizens who have not interacted directly with police trained in ways designed to enhance perceptions of procedural justice.

Recommendation: All officers, shacham, and volunteers should be trained to interact with citizens in ways that enhance procedural justice. This includes explaining procedures, treating all members of the public with respect, listening and responding to concerns raised by citizens, treating all members of the public equally and fairly, and exhibiting minimum standards of knowledge and competence.

Train and Manage Police Volunteers

Although the focus groups we conducted raised questions about the apparent professionalism of the Israel Police, we were unable to distinguish between perceptions of full-time police and perceptions of shacham and volunteers. Anecdotal evidence suggests the Israeli public has the same difficulty, in that both dress in a manner indistinguishable from professional police. This is a serious problem for the police because of the large numbers of volunteers, the lower standards of training to which volunteers and shacham are held, and the high levels of responsibility they are given. Shacham and volunteers may detract from the professional image and performance standards the Israel Police strives to maintain. Several steps should be taken to make better, more efficient use of volunteers, while ensuring that they are not put in positions where their inexperience and lack of formal training will reflect poorly on the entirety of the Israel Police.

The issue of volunteers in Israel is complex and owes as much to history, external threats, and social norms as to considerations of policing effectiveness. Social goals other than straight policing outcomes may be served by this program. Political attitudes might also militate against abridging this aspect of citizen volunteerism. For these reasons, it is especially important for the police to develop a clear mission statement and goals for the use of a volunteer police force. This should include a clear statement regarding the purpose of the volunteer force, the types of activities that are appropriate for volunteers, and the structure of the volunteer force. The police should consider how the volunteers will enhance the effectiveness of the police force.

In developing the mission and goals, the Israel Police should gather information from multiple sources, including current volunteers, community members, and the regular police. Information from these different sources can help identify what activities may be most appropriate for the range of skills volunteers might bring, identify needs of the community, and determine how police think volunteers might be best integrated into their activities. Involving police in defining the mission and goals is particularly important for establishing police acceptance.

Already, Israel Police volunteers are differentiated in terms of those who perform elite functions and those who provide other types of services. There is value in distinguishing between volunteer positions that have high expectations for attendance and performance and those that do not. A group of elite, highly trained, and well-screened volunteers can serve as an official part of the police force with some legitimate authority over the public. But principles of effective human resource management should be employed for both these volunteers and those fulfilling less demanding functions. The best avenues for preventing abuses and for encouraging good performance among volunteers are no different from those that should be applied to the rest of the police force.[1] This includes screening out people who are not qualified; pro-

---

[1] For more on the fundamentals of effective human resource practices, see Anderson et al. (2002).

viding appropriate training and development; and providing supervision, performance feedback, and accountability, as well as rewards for model behavior. Regardless of the level of direct supervision, all volunteers need to be held accountable for their actions. For all volunteers, the Israel Police should communicate performance expectations and provide feedback. For those in more-elite positions with time commitments, the police should also hold regular performance evaluations.

For the police not only to manage this resource more effectively but also to provide a basis for explaining to others what the appropriate nature and degree of involvement of volunteers in policing missions are, the effectiveness of both volunteers and shacham should be monitored and evaluated continually. We recommend drawing data from several sources, including surveys and interviews of volunteers, reactions of community groups, records of public complaints, and interviews with police directly engaged in supervising volunteers and with the police force as a whole.

We also note that, among the volunteer forces we analyzed, only those in South Africa wear a uniform indistinguishable from that of the police. In an environment where confusion already exists over what the police role should be, as well as a perception of great variability of the performance of individual police officers, it may be appropriate for the police to consider whether this policy of perceived seamlessness between professional police and volunteers truly serves the police as an organization or the country in assuring its citizens of the capabilities of those they perceive as being sworn officers.

Recommendation: Develop a clear mission statement and goals for the use of a volunteer police force. Follow key principles of effective human resource management by screening candidates for elite volunteer jobs; matching skills to job requirements; establishing training programs for volunteers; and providing supervision, performance feedback, and accountability. Evaluate the need for a distinguishing uniform. Both the volunteer and shacham programs should be monitored and evaluated for effectiveness.

Apply a Strategic Perspective to Police Personnel Requirements

RAND was not asked to address personnel issues directly. Yet several of the efforts, such as the benchmarking of Israel Police resources, the implementation of procedural justice, and comparisons with other forces in the use of police volunteers, led indirectly to personnel issues. We are not in a position to recommend, for example, that the police significantly increase the use of civilians, previously never greater than 5 percent of Israel Police total personnel and well below the 25 to 35 percent found in most U.S. police departments.[2] The requirements of the Israel Police are different, for example, in the role played and the need to mobilize in the face of national emergencies. Similarly, we have no basis for judging the appropriate level and role of volunteers in carrying out the broad range of policing missions in Israel. But the police would be well served in putting themselves in a position to make such assessments.

Police staffing should be in accordance with the goals that Israel expects its police to achieve, the missions they are asked to carry out, and the activities they engage in to carry out these missions and achieve these goals. Issues of appropriate numbers, categories of personnel, and employment conditions can only be determined on this basis if the Israel Police are to maintain the effectiveness that they expect from themselves.

In particular, the police should consider a careful analysis of police job functions, to possibly realign personnel resources with departmental strategic objectives. Such a job function analysis should consider

- experience and aptitude requirements for eligibility for different jobs
- minimum initial and ongoing training requirements
- whether the function is better performed by a sworn officer or civilian
- whether the function is appropriate for a volunteer or shacham

---

[2]   The Law Enforcement Management and Administrative Statistics series shows that about one-third of employees in U.S. local police and sheriffs departments were civilians in 2007. See U.S. Department of Justice, 2007, p. 8.

- selection and promotion procedures.

Recommendation: The Israel Police should carry out a job analysis designed to align job functions, training, qualifications, and selection procedures with police goals, missions, and strategies.

Improving Policing Deterrence

Table 4.4 summarizes our recommendations for improving policing deterrence.

Design Focused Deterrence Interventions

Earlier in this report, we described the low value of general deterrence methods that did not target a specific crime problem. However, focused deterrence efforts have some prospect for improving the Israel Police's standing with the public. Focused deterrence, when conducted properly, involves forming partnerships with community members and organizations and can necessitate structural realignments to be effective. In short, focused deterrence activities can be supportive of, and an important component of, community policing.

In Chapter Three, we discussed the SARA approach as an example of problem-oriented policing that also has implications for both deterrence and community policing. Crucially, SARA employs data, analysis, and measured assessment of outcomes. By its nature, SARA tends to focus on problems at the community level (or below). This in turn means that SARA-type interventions allow for evaluation of police

Table 4.4
Recommendations: Policing Deterrence

Area	Recommendation
Deterrence	• Design focused deterrence interventions and reduce reliance on procedures that are rooted in general deterrence theories
Organizational learning	• Develop a best practices database for focused deterrence methods and procedures in Israel

effectiveness at the community (or subnational) level. Police effectiveness at resolving community concerns should be a focus of such deterrence interventions. The SARA approach has been used against a wide variety of problems, including the operation of open-air drug markets, homeless encampments in urban areas, bicycle theft, neighborhood noise, and gang crime (Center for Problem-Oriented Policing, 2011). Many accessible and helpful training materials for police departments are widely available (Clarke and Eck, 2003).

Recommendation: Develop a plan to institutionalize the SARA (or other research-based) approach at the district or subdistrict level. Create a national deterrence program oversight team and deterrence research team to ensure that proposed interventions are responsive to public needs, are based on careful empirical analysis of the problem, receive tailored interventions designed to address the specific problem, and are subjected to careful evaluation and appropriate in-process adjustments.

Develop a Best Practices Database

A policing organization that orients itself toward problem-oriented policing methods, such as SARA, must become a learning organization if it is going to carry out these strategies successfully at an operational level. The extraordinary efforts the Israel Police has already made to integrate data on activities, performance, and results put it in a good position to go one step further and entertain the possibility of creating its own internal best-practices archive to reinforce the productivity of operations throughout the country. The level of organization inherent in the previous recommendation would provide a basis for doing so.

Recommendation: Document all results—effective and ineffective. The national deterrence oversight team should review research evidence and recommend best practices to help ensure that resources are used effectively when or if the problem reoccurs or develops in another part of the country.

Next Steps

We believe that all our recommendations are important elements for ensuring that effective policing prevails in Israel. They may appear daunting in their totality. However, all are amenable to phased introduction over time. In many cases, there are both near-term and long-term components. We illustrate this point by suggesting specific steps to implement our two keystone recommendations to establish a procedural justice model for policing in Israel and to shift toward a posture of focused, rather than general, deterrence.

Table 4.5 shows both immediate and longer-term actions for creating a procedural justice model. The steps are derived directly from our recommendations. Table 4.6 does the same for focused deterrence.

Table 4.5
Steps for Adopting a Procedural Justice Model

Outcome	Short-Term Actions	Longer-Term Actions
Ensure that all procedures are fair, unbiased, and transparent	Review and standardize policies and procedures	Release policies and procedures to the public to demonstrate they are fair
	Change policies and procedures that are biased	Create system to allow public to better monitor crime and police activity; incorporate into Mifne
	Review training and ensure that police standardize their procedures	
Take steps to administer procedures in a fair, unbiased, and transparent way	Train police to administer fair, unbiased, and transparent treatment	Release data on policies and procedures to demonstrate they are being implemented in a fair, unbiased way
	Monitor actions on the street	Release data on individual police accountability; incorporate measures into Mifne
	Create a system of rewards and punishments to incentivize police to use standards	

Table 4.6
Steps for Adopting Focused Deterrence

Outcome	Short-Term Actions	Longer-Term Actions
Create new SARA-based deterrence focus at the district, subdistrict, or station level	Form new team to create and oversee project	Conduct research on effectiveness of different deterrence projects
	Train commanders in SARA (or other research-based problem-solving procedure)	Incorporate measures into Mifne
	Submit proposals and hold commanders accountable	
Create a research-based best practices database	Collect data from all projects to identify which projects, and which project components, are successful	Disseminate information on effective programs
		Encourage commanders to use effective practices identified in research
		Incorporate measure into Mifne

It is our conclusion that taking these steps will provide both Israel and its police with meaningful assurance that policing effectiveness may be enhanced and maintained in the years to come.

CHAPTER FIVE

Conclusion: Embracing a New Posture for Policing in Israel

There is a mismatch today between what the Israel Police does and what the public expects of it. To the degree this stems from misunderstanding, improved public information about police success and examples of heroism and sacrifice might have an effect, as would better awareness of police policies and procedures. Some in the Israel Police have argued, however, that there are important opportunities for the Israel Police to bring its activities and culture into better alignment with the expectations of a wider segment of the community. Moreover, such efforts are likely to increase the success of the police not just in terms of public satisfaction, but also in terms of the cooperation the police receive in pursuing investigations, the respect officers are accorded as they perform their duties, and the quality of officers and staff who can be recruited to the force.

This report has provided a series of recommendations that arose from the analyses we conducted, our observation and discussion of police practice in Israel, and the relevant experience of other police forces. The overall intent is to enhance the effectiveness of policing in Israel in the fullest sense of the word. These recommendations are mutually supporting and should be considered together. As such, they fall under two main headings:

- embracing a procedural justice model for serving and interacting with the Israeli public while carrying out police activities

- expanding the use of information to support more focused deterrence and police activity and less reliance on a posture of general deterrence.

Procedural justice is a general term for policing practices that ensure that interactions with the police are perceived as fair and just. This means developing policing standards and a police culture that provides consistency in the treatment of citizens without regard either to who an individual is or which officer responds to a call. It means treating citizens with respect and dignity, such as listening and trying to understand citizens' perspectives on the problem, explaining procedures and progress, and providing timely and accurate information. One finding of our research is that there is a widely held perception, and not only in Israel's minority communities, that this is not currently the case. We find in this a significant contributing factor to many of the more specific complaints and frictions that arise between Israel's police and the communities that they serve. We also point out that the communities themselves can become partners with the police in effecting the change that would be required.

We also found that in Israel, as elsewhere, the general approach to deterrence of crime is rarely as effective or efficient in the use of resources as more focused deterrence that makes the fullest use of information and analysis to apply policing resources to specific problems and goals. The police in Israel already possess extraordinary potential for deploying existing assets in a way that can take fullest advantage of its abilities for gathering and assessing data.

Fully realizing this potential will also not simply be a matter of changing emphases and procedures. As with other policing organizations that have shifted toward this posture for deterrence, the Israel Police may find it of value to draw on the assistance of external academic or analytical institutions to supplement its own abilities to conduct and apply the necessary analyses. But it will also require substantial change in the culture of the organization and the extent of integration across different divisions and between the field and headquarters leadership.

Figure 5.1 shows how the emphases on procedural justice and a focused deterrence program may affect the two main drivers of perceived police effectiveness: public support and policing outcomes. The figure also shows the main elements for establishing such emphasis.

Effecting far-reaching changes to the culture and performance of any policing organization poses a major challenge and is unlikely to succeed without strong leadership support, objective performance standards and measures, hiring strategies and training standards that guarantee necessary levels of competence in new policing requirements, and external accountability. The fact that the Israel Police and its partnering ministries initiated the project we describe in this report; were willing to engage in a broad and detailed examination of so many aspects of policing; and, during the course of our work, have already shown an inclination toward transformation and change suggests that the police and their governmental partners are ready to meet these challenges.

Figure 5.1
The Role of Procedural Justice and Focused Deterrence in Police Effectiveness

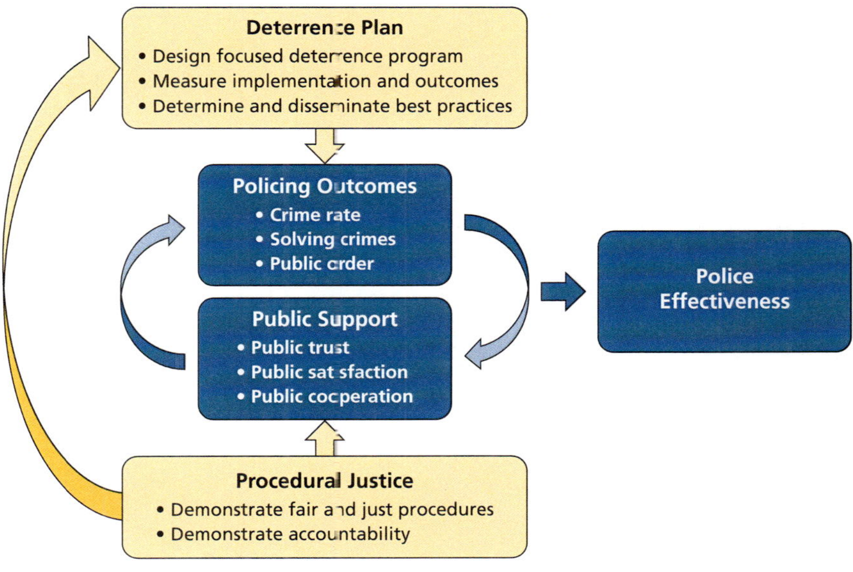

References

Abadie, Alberto, Alexis Diamond, and Jens Hainmueller, "Synthetic Control Methods for Comparative Case Studies: Estimating the Effect of California's Tobacco Control Program," *Journal of the American Statistical Association*, Vol. 105, No. 490, June 2010, pp. 493–505.

Anderson, Niel, Deniz S. Ones, Handan Kepir Sinangil, and Chockalingam Viswesvaran, eds., *Handbook of Industrial, Work, and Organizational Psychology*, Vol. 1, *Personnel Psychology*, Thousand Oaks, Calif.: Sage Publications, 2002.

Ayling, Julie, "Force Multiplier: People as a Policing Resource," *International Journal of Comparative and Applied Criminal Justice*, Vol. 32, No. 1, January 2007, pp. 73–100.

Bayley, David H., "Law Enforcement and the Rule of Law: Is There a Tradeoff?" *Criminology and Public Policy*, Vol. 2, No. 1, November 2002, pp. 133–154.

Ben-Porat, Guy, and Fanny Yuval, "The Police and Arab Society in Israel: Opinions, Expectations, and Needs," in Besorah Rogev, ed., *Leading Research Findings 2009: Research Papers and Literature Review About Policing Practice in Israel* [in Hebrew], Jerusalem: Israel Police Division of Planning and Organization, 2009, pp. 133–143.

Ben-Porat, Guy, and Fanny Yuval, "Minorities in Democracy and Policing Policy: From Alienation to Cooperation," *Policing and Society*, Vol. 22, No. 2, November 2011.

Birzer Michael L., "The Theory of Andragogy Applied to Police Training," *Policing: An International Journal of Police Strategies and Management*, Vol. 26, No. 1, 2003.

Blakemore, Jerome L., David Barlow, and Deborah L. Padgett, "From the Classroom to the Community: Introducing Process in Police Diversity Training," *Police Studies*, Vol. 18, No. 1, 1995, pp. 71–83.

Bowling, Ben, and Coretta Phillips, "Policing Ethnic Minority Communities," in Tim Newburn, ed., *Handbook of Policing*, Devon, UK: Willan Publishing, 2003, pp. 528–555.

Brown, Ben, and Wm. Reed Benedict, "Perceptions of the Police: Past Findings, Methodological Issues, Conceptual Issues and Policy Implications," *Policing: An International Journal of Police Strategies and Management*, Vol. 25, No. 3, 2002, pp. 543–580.

Center for Problem-Oriented Policing, "Goldstein Awards 2011," web page, 2011. As of January 10, 2013:
http://www.popcenter.org/library/awards/goldstein.cfm?browse=abstracts&year=2011

Centre of Excellence in Policing and Security, Queensland Community Engagement Trial (QCET), website, 2013. As of January 18, 2013:
http://www.ceps.edu.au/programs/vulnerable-communities/queensland-community-engagement-trial--qcet-

Clarke, Ronald V., and John E. Eck, *Become a Problem Solving Crime Analyst: In 55 Small Steps*, London: Jill Dando Institute of Crime Science, University College, 2003. As of January 11, 2013:
http://www.popcenter.org/library/reading/pdfs/55stepsUK.pdf

Cochran, Joshua C., and Patricia Y. Warren, "Racial, Ethnic, and Gender Differences in Perceptions of the Police: The Salience of Officer Race Within the Context of Racial Profiling," *Journal of Contemporary Criminal Justice*, Vol. 28, No. 2, May 2012, pp. 206–277.

Davids, Cindy, *Conflict of Interest in Policing: Problems, Practices, and Principles*, Sydney: Sydney Institute of Criminology Monograph Series, No. 26, 2008.

Davis, R. C., G. Cordner, C. Hartley, R. Newell, and C. Ortiz, *Striving for Excellence: Technical Report on Field Testing a Suite of Standardized Performance Measures*, Washington, D.C.: Bureau of Justice Assistance, U.S. Department of Justice, 2010.

Davis, Robert C., and Nicole J. Hendricks, "Immigrants and Law Enforcement: A Comparison of Native-Born and Foreign-Born Americans' Opinions of the Police," *International Review of Victimology*, Vol. 14, No. 1, January 2007, pp. 81–94.

European Social Survey, website, 2012. As of January 11, 2013:
http://www.europeansocialsurvey.org/

Gaston, Kevin, and Jackie A. Alexander, "Effective Organisation and Management of Public Sector Volunteer Workers: Police Special Constables," *International Journal of Public Sector Management*, Vol. 14, No. 1, 2001, pp. 59–74.

Gould, Larry, "Can an Old Dog Be Taught New Tricks? Teaching Cultural Diversity to Police Officers," *Policing: An International Journal of Police Strategies and Management*, Vol. 20, No. 2, 1997, pp. 339–356.

Graber, Doris A., *Crime News and the Public*, New York: Praeger, 1980.

Graduate Institute of International Studies, *Small Arms Survey 2007: Guns and the City*, Cambridge, UK.: Cambridge University Press, 2007.

Hasisi, Badi, and Ronald Weitzer, "Police Relations with Arabs and Jews in Israel," *British Journal of Criminology*, Vol. 47, No. 5, September 2007, pp. 728–745.

Hermann, Tamar, Nir Atmor, Ella Heller, and Yuval Lebel, *Israel Democracy Index 2012*, Jerusalem: Israel Democracy Institute, 2012.

Hinds, Lyn, "Youth, Police Legitimacy and Informal Contact," *Journal of Police and Criminal Psychology*, Vol. 24 No. 1, March 2009, pp. 10–21.

Home Office (United Kingdom), *Building Communities, Beating Crime: A Better Police Service for the 21st Century*, November 2004. As of January 16, 2013: http://www.archive2.official-documents.co.uk/document/cm63/6360/6360.pdf

Ivkovic, Sanja Kutnjak, and Tara O'Connor Shelley, "The Contours of Police Integrity Across Eastern Europe: The Case of Bosnia and Herzegovina and the Czech Republic," *International Criminal Justice Review*, Vol. 18, No. 1, March 2008, pp. 59–82.

Klockars, Carl B., Sanja Kutnjak Ivkovich, and Maria R. Haberfeld, *Enhancing Police Integrity*, Washington, D.C.: National Institute of Justice, December 2005.

Klockars, Carl B., Sanja Kutnjak Ivkovich, William E. Harver, and Maria R. Haberfeld, *The Measurement of Police Integrity*, Washington, D.C.: National Institute of Justice, May 2000.

Macpherson, William, "The Stephen Lawrence Inquiry: Report of an Inquiry by Sir William Macpherson of Cluny," London: The Stationary Office, February 1999. As of January 10, 2013: http://www.archive.official-documents.co.uk/document/cm42/4262/4262.htm

Maguire, Edward, and William Wells, *Implementing Community Policing: Lessons from 12 Agencies*, Washington, D.C.: Office of Community Oriented Policing Services, 2009.

Mastrofski, Stephen D., "Policing for People," *Ideas in American Policing*, March 1999. As of January 18, 2013: http://www.policefoundation.org/content/policing-people

McCombs, Maxwell, *Setting the Agenda: The Mass Media and Public Opinion*, Cambridge, UK: Polity Press, 2004.

Miller, Joel, Robert C. Davis, Nicole J. Henderson, John Markovic, and Christopher Ortiz, "Measuring Influences on Public Opinion of the Police Using Time-Series Data: Results of a Pilot Study," *Police Quarterly*, Vol. 8, No. 3, 2005, pp. 394–401.

Murphy, Kristina, and Adrian Cherney, "Understanding Cooperation with Police in a Diverse Society," *British Journal of Criminology*, Vol. 52, No. 1, January 2012, pp. 181–201.

Northern Ireland Policing Board, "Policing and Community Safety Partnerships," web page, 2012. As of January 10, 2013:
http://www.nipolicingboard.org.uk/index/our-work/policing_and_community_safety_partnerships.htm

Pelfrey, William V., Jr., "The Inchoate Nature of Community Policing: Differences Between Community Policing and Traditional Police Officers," *Justice Quarterly*, Vol. 21, No. 3, September 2004, pp. 579–601.

Rain, John W., and Eileen Dunstan, "Enhancing Accountability in Local Policing," *Policing*, Vol. 1, No. 3, 2007, pp. 327–341.

Reaves, Brian A., *Local Police Departments, 2007*, Bureau of Justice Statistics, NCJ 231174, December 2, 2010. As of January 11, 2013:
http://bjs.ojp.usdoj.gov/index.cfm?ty=pbdetail&iid=1750

Reisig, Michael, "Procedural Justice and Community Policing—What Shapes Residents' Willingness to Participate in Crime Prevention Programs?" *Policing*, Vol. 1, No. 3, 2007, pp. 356–369.

Ridgeway, Greg, *Analysis of Racial Disparities in the New York Police Department's Stop, Question, and Frisk Practices*, Santa Monica, Calif.: RAND Corporation, TR-534-NYCPF, 2007. As of May 22, 2013:
http://www.rand.org/pubs/technical_reports/TR534.html

Ridgeway, Greg, Terry L. Schell, Brian Gifford, Jessica Saunders, Susan Turner, K. Jack Riley, and Travis L. Dixon, *Police-Community Relations in Cincinnati*, Santa Monica, Calif.: RAND Corporation, MG-853-CC, 2009. As of January 10, 2013:
http://www.rand.org/pubs/monographs/MG853.html

Rogev, Besorah, ed., *Leading Research Findings 2009: Research Papers and Literature Review About Policing Practice in Israel* [in Hebrew], Jerusalem: Israel Police Division of Planning and Organization, 2009.

Rosenbaum, Dennis P., Amie M. Schuck, Sandra K. Costello, Darnell F. Hawkins, and Marianne K. Ring, "Attitudes Toward the Police: The Effects of Direct and Vicarious Experience," *Police Quarterly*, Vol. 8, No. 3, September 2005, pp. 343–365.

Sauerman, Adri, and Sanja Kutnjak Ivkovich, "Measuring the Integrity of the South African Police Service During Transitional Times," *Acta Criminologica*, Vol. 2, 2008, pp. 21–39.

Sozer, Mehmet Alper, and Alida V. Merlo, "The Impact of Community Policing on Crime Rates: Does the Effect of Community Policing Differ in Large and Small Law Enforcement Agencies?" *Police Practice and Research*, February 2012, pp. 1–16.

Stenning, Philip C., "Policing the Cultural Kaleidoscope: Recent Canadian Experience," *Police and Society*, No. 7, 2003, pp. 13–47.

Tita, George, K. Jack Riley, Greg Ridgeway, Clifford A. Grammich, Allan Abrahamse, and Peter W. Greenwood, *Reducing Gun Violence: Results from an Intervention in East Los Angeles*, Santa Monica, Calif.: RAND Corporation, MR-1764-1-NIJ, 2003. As of January 211, 2013:
http://www.rand.org/pubs/monograph_reports/MR1764-1.html

Topping, John R., "Diversifying from Within: Community Policing and the Governance of Security in Northern Ireland," *British Journal of Criminology*, Vol. 48, No. 6, 2008, pp. 778–797.

Tyler, Tom R., "Enhancing Police Legitimacy," *Annals of the American Academy of Political and Social Science*, Vol. 593, No. 1, 2004, pp. 84–99.

Tyler, Tom R., and Cheryl J. Wakslak, "Profiling and Police Legitimacy: Procedural Justice, Attributions of Motive, and Acceptance of Police Authority," *Criminology*, Vol. 42, No. 2, May 2004, pp. 253–281.

U.S. Department of Justice, "Community Policing Defined," Community Oriented Policing Services website, undated. As of January 10, 2013:
http://www.cops.usdoj.gov/default.asp?item=36

U.S. Department of Justice, Office of Justice Programs, Bureau of Justice Statistics, *Law Enforcement Management and Administrative Statistics (LEMAS), 2007* [Computer file], Ann Arbor, Mich.: Inter-University Consortium for Political and Social Research [distributor], ICPSR31161-v1, 2007. As of May 22, 2013:
http://www.icpsr.umich.edu/icps-web/NACJD/series/92/studies/31161

Vigoda, Eran, and Shlomo Mizrachi, *Israel Public Sector Performance: Survey of Citizens and National Estimates 2012* [in Hebrew], Beersheva: Guilford Glazer School of Business and Management, Ben-Gurion University of the Negev, 2012.

Wakefield, Alison, "Carry on Constable? Revaluing Foot Patrol," *Policing*, Vol. 1, No. 3, September 2007, pp. 342–355.

Walker, Samuel, *The New World of Police Accountability*, Thousand Oaks, Calif.: Sage Publications, 2005.

Walker, Samuel, Geoffrey P. Alpert, and Dennis J. Kenney, *Early Warning Systems: Responding to the Problem Police Officer*, National Institute of Justice Research Brief, July 2001.

Weitzer, Ronald, "Incidents of Police Misconduct and Public Opinion," *Journal of Criminal Justice*, Vol. 30, No. 5, September–October 2002, pp. 397–408.

Weitzer, Ronald, and Badi Hasisi, "Does Ethnic Composition Make a Difference? Citizens' Assessments of Arab Police Officers In Israel," *Policing and Society*, Vol. 18, No. 4, December 2008, pp. 362–376.

Weitzer, Ronald, and Steven A. Tuch, "Perceptions of Racial Profiling: Race, Class and Personal Experience," *Criminology*, Vol. 40, No. 2, May 2002, pp. 435–456.

Wilson, Jeremy M., and Amy G. Cox, *Community Policing and Crime: The Process and Impact of Problem-Solving in Oakland*, Santa Monica, Calif.: RAND Corporation, TR-635-BPA, 2008. As of January 11, 2013:
http://www.rand.org/pubs/technical_reports/TR635.html

Yanay, Uri, "Co-Opting Vigilantism: Government Response to Community Action for Personal Safety," *Journal of Public Policy*, Vol. 13, No. 4, October 1993, pp. 381–396.

Yanich, Danilo, *Crime, Community and Local TV News: Covering Crime in Philadelphia and Baltimore*, Newark, Del.: Center for Community Development and Family Policy and Center on Crime, Communities and Culture, University of Delaware, 1998.

Yogev, Dikla, *Public Attitudes Toward the Israel Police 2010* [in Hebrew], Tel Aviv: Ministry of Public Security, 2010.